Life Cycle Costing: A Better Method of Government Procurement

Other Titles in This Series

Westview Special Studies in Public Policy and Public Systems Management

Life Cycle Costing:
A Better Method of Government Procurement
M. Robert Seldon

Life Cycle Costing (LCC) is a procurement method that takes into account the total cost of product development, procurement, and ownership, recognizing that purchase price may be less significant than subsequent ownership costs. As the Department of Defense and other federal agencies seek to lower costs in a time of tight budgets, LCC has become an important government procurement strategy.

This book explains how both government procurement agencies and industrial contractors can effectively use LCC. The author analyzes the effects of inflation and discounting, describes cost models and computer methods for selecting the best of several alternative procurements, and demonstrates the effective application of these methods to optimize a project's life cycle cost. Specific management controls, audits, and presentations are given, along with suggestions for practical use.

The book ends with a discussion of strategies that will help buyers obtain the lowest life cycle costs and contractors win in a competitive market. There is also an extensive bibliography.

M. Robert Seldon, chief of life cycle costing at General Dynamics Corporation, has applied the LCC method for several major U.S. government defense programs. He has worked in the areas of reliability, maintainability, and logistics technology at General Dynamics, in quality assurance at LTV, Inc., and at NASA.

Life Cycle Costing: A Better Method of Government Procurement

M. Robert Seldon

Westview Press / Boulder, Colorado

Westview Special Studies in Public Policy
and Public Systems Management

Copyright © 1979 by Westview Press, Inc.

Published in 1979 in the United States of America by
Westview Press, Inc.
5500 Central Avenue
Boulder, Colorado 80301
Frederick A. Praeger, Publisher

Library of Congress Cataloging in Publication Data
Seldon, M. Robert.
Life cycle costing.
(Westview special studies in public policy and public systems management)
Bibliography: p.
1. Government purchasing—United States—Cost effectiveness. 2. United States
—Armed Forces—Procurement—Cost effectiveness. I. Title.
JK1673.S44   353.007'12   78-15446
ISBN 0-89158-277-0

Printed and bound in the United States of America

To Mervyn,
who made this book possible

Contents

Figures

Tables

Preface

This book provides step-by-step methods for the use of life cycle cost (LCC) in all phases of planning and procurement. Government procurement, particularly military procurement (where LCC started), is the book's principal emphasis, but the methods it describes are widely applicable in business and industry. The relationships between design and cost are presented and integrated with the LCC approach.

Both buyers and sellers should use life cycle costing, and this book discusses the concerns and problems of the two parties. It is intended for the LCC analyst who deals with the practical problems of preparing LCC requirements and estimates on a day-to-day basis; for the systems engineer and designer who must balance cost considerations with performance; and for the manager who must integrate LCC with all the complex problems of procurement and/or sales.

The LCC estimates developed by the methods in this book are particularly useful in cost-effectiveness and cost-benefit studies. The evaluation of performance, effectiveness, benefits, or other measures of success in filling a mission need is ouside of the scope of this book.

The first five chapters of the book outline the use of LCC and methods for estimating research and development costs, production costs, operating and support costs, and miscellaneous costs and revenue. Even those familiar with estimating methods should review these chapters because they explain the scope of LCC and introduce some important ideas, such as the use of work breakdown structures, cost breakdown structures, and risk analysis. In particular, the estimation of operating and support costs in Chapter 4 is central to LCC (methods of controlling such costs during the development process are discussed in Chapter 9).

The next four chapters discuss the intricacies of various methods of estimating LCC. Chapter 6 provides methods of handling inflation and the time value of money. Contractual techniques for controlling LCC are the subject of Chapter 7. The use of data in LCC estimates requires an orderly structure for conceptual consistency and for mechanical accuracy; various models and their desirable characteristics are discussed in Chapter 8. As mentioned above, Chapter 9 follows LCC through the development process to assure that product design integrates costing with other considerations.

The last two chapters consider management problems. Chapter 10 discusses ways to review and control the LCC process, and Chapter 11 proposes management strategies that both buyer and seller can use to maximum benefit.

After completing the book, readers should review the planning ideas suggested in Chapter 1, for these are designed to provide guidelines for actual life cycle costing operations. Other chapters in the book should continue to be useful to those who have mastered LCC methods both for reference purposes and for the clarification of specific problems.

*   *   *

I am grateful for the support of my employer, the General Dynamics Corporation, during the writing of this book. I should also like to express my thanks to the many co-workers and associates who helped by answering my numerous questions. A few merit special recognition, even at the risk of seeming ingratitude in the omission of many others: Grant Gabel, Gary Glenn, and James Styerwalt were particularly helpful. My appreciation also goes to my fellow students and the faculty at Claremont Graduate School. In particular, Professors Peter F. Drucker and James P. Giles provided invaluable advice and encouragement. I am indebted to my publisher, Frederick A. Praeger, his executive editor Lynne Rienner, and most importantly to my editor, M. W. A. Seldon. My gratitude goes to all those who so generously gave of their time. Any remaining errors, omissions, and problems are, of course, my responsibility.

M. Robert Seldon

1
An Introduction to
Life Cycle Costing

Federal, state, and local governments have customarily sought to buy the least expensive product available. When holding a contract competition among manufacturers, the government has generally chosen the lowest bidder. There have been exceptions to this rule, of course. Sometimes the government has selected a higher-priced product on grounds of superior performance. On other occasions, factors such as a contractor's delivery schedule, his use of standardized components, and his past record have influenced the purchasing decision. In recent years, as budgets have become tighter, the federal government, led by the Department of Defense (DOD), has realized that the purchase price of the product represents only part of its total or life cycle cost. Ownership costs—those of operation and support or maintenance—have frequently far exceeded procurement costs and have therefore imposed strict limits on the amount of equipment that could be afforded. For example, as Figure 1-1 shows, operation and support costs consumed 53 percent of the 1979 DOD budget.[1] The military services particularly have been troubled about the expense of training and retaining skilled manpower for operation and maintenance of complex equipment. As a result, the DOD has become aware that a low purchase price frequently means high operation and

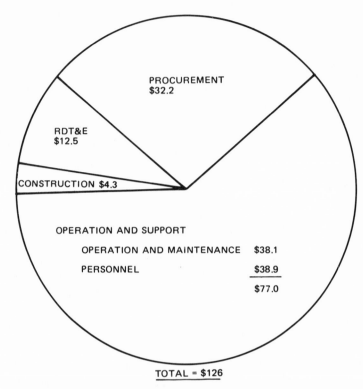

Figure 1-1. Department of Defense 1979 Budget
Billions of Dollars

support costs and has moved toward making the total cost of
equipment by the end of its life cycle the preeminent selection factor. This concept is known as life cycle cost (LCC).

The concept of LCC was initiated by the Department of
Defense and first used in its procurement in the early 1960s.
Today, various directives and instructions have formalized
the policy,[2] which has been adopted by other agencies as a
procurement criterion and endorsed by the Congress.[3] The
main motivation behind LCC is the possibility of saving
money on operating and support costs by spending somewhat
more during research and development and, therefore, in
procurement cost. A second motivation is to encourage long-

range planning, especially for operation and support costs. The selection of the lowest purchase price is now seen as false economy, and LCC is regarded as a better criterion than purchase price for government procurement. The LCC estimating process provides all management with an overall quantitative picture of the life cycle of an item and particularly enhances contractor interest in operation and support plans, which are usually a vague and unimportant consideration during the early phases of planning and may be neglected as well during the later phases of development. Such management interest in, and attention to, the user's problems invariably results in improved design for the user.

Because new military equipment is usually innovative, complex, and expensive, the military services (and for similar reasons, other government agencies) have often found it hard to estimate life cycle costs. Nevertheless, the increased attention paid to LCC in procurement decisions has gradually made the techniques for determining life cycle cost more accurate, reliable, and systematic. The purpose of this book, therefore, is to explain how these techniques can best be applied—by both government procurement personnel and contractors—at each stage of the procurement process. This chapter discusses the problems LCC has faced and provides an overview of the LCC process. The next four chapters explain methods of calculating the LCC of items from the earliest phase of research and development through the final computations of salvage price at the end of a product's lifetime. Chapters 6 through 10 then discuss some advanced techniques of life cycle costing, and a concluding chapter examines management strategy for LCC and the outlook for the future.

Of course, LCC also has many uses outside the government and the defense industry. For many years, astute managements of industrial and commercial firms have weighed ownership costs of various capital investment strategies before reaching an investment decision.[4] At a lower level,

LCC calculations are as applicable to the choice between a diesel and a gasoline-powered automobile as they are to the choice between a diesel-powered and a gasoline-powered tank. Thus, many of the LCC methods explained in this book have civilian as well as military applications. Generally, however, the discussion here applies to a monopsony, where there is but one buyer and many sellers.

Resistances to LCC

In recent years, the many advantages of LCC have led such agencies as the Congress, the Department of Defense, and the General Services Administration (GSA) to advocate its use, and many contractors have also developed expertise in this area. If small additional acquisition costs can yield significant reductions in operating and maintenance costs and if LCC is an important planning tool, why have so few procurements been contracted on an LCC basis? Five factors explain the resistance to the concept.

1. *Congress votes separate appropriations of procurement funds and operating and maintenance funds.* As a result, responsibility for the administration of procurement funds has been separated from that for the administration of operating and maintenance funds. Thus, there is no institutional incentive for a procurement organization to pay a higher purchase price for an item in order to decrease later costs for the product's operation and support.

The original intent of the Congress was to designate and control expenditures by specifying the use of appropriated funds. However, if an agency can show the Congress, even after the appropriation is made, that a reallocation would result in economies, Congress will reconsider. The Senate Subcommittee on Federal Spending Practices, Efficiency, and Open Government has stated, "DOD is permitted to re-program from one program element to another as the need arises, unencumbered by high level procedural approval, as long as the program element cost that contains the projects does not exceed its allocation by more than $2 million."[5] In relation to most DOD projects, this is a fairly small concession, but the senators clearly understand the problem and are willing to assist the DOD in the optimum allocation of funds. Other appropriating legislators can be shown that such flexibility benefits all parties. As more agencies use LCC and present the logic and conclusions to the Congress, such flexibility will be even more evident. Top level managements are therefore urging their organizations to perform trade-offs between procurement and operating and maintenance funds. The tight compartments and insular thinking of separate organizations are breaking down.

2. *LCC has encountered political objections to front-end loading: higher initial costs in research, development, and production in order to achieve later economies in operation and support.* Immediate budget stringencies often exert a much stronger influence on politicians than anticipated savings in an uncertain future. The Congress and the administration believe that the public judges them on the basis of their current performance, not on the possible benefits resulting from their long-range planning.

There is abundant evidence, however, that congressmen and senators are not nearly so shortsighted as conventional wisdom holds. Despite the pressure to get reelected on the basis of performance during the current session, many recent congressional debates have shown that members of Congress do try to take a conscientious, longer view.[6] When the DOD or some other agency has clearly presented the alternatives, the Congress has opted for the lower total cost, not just for the lower immediate cost. Management at other levels of government (and industry) is following these examples and taking a longer-range view.

3. *Some past procurement policies resembling LCC have turned out badly.* During the 1960s, then Secretary of Defense Robert S. McNamara (1961-1968) instituted several

major "total package procurements," which incurred widespread criticism for their heavy cost overruns. The most notorious of these was the C-5A transport aircraft; others were the short-range, air-launched missile (SRAM), the Cheyenne helicopter, and the F-14 fighter plane.[7] Total package procurement attempted to contract for the total cost of development and production early in the development cycle and did not explicitly concern itself with later phases, whereas LCC seeks to evaluate (and later contract for) the costs of procurement _and_ operation and maintenance. Despite these crucial differences, LCC has had to bear the onus for the failure of total package procurement and has therefore been adopted slowly.

Recent DOD and congressional actions indicate that memories of these traumas are fading. For example, the contract award for the F-16 lightweight fighter aircraft included LCC requirements for a reliability improvement warranty, target logistic support, cost contractual requirements, and a large LCC analysis task (see Chapter 7 for a discussion of these provisions). Moreover, the contract went to General Dynamics Corporation, the producer of the F-111 aircraft, an exemplar of the McNamara era. Today, as the DOD gains confidence in LCC methods, it is writing an increasing number of contracts with LCC provisions.

4. _There are doubts about the accuracy and reliability of data and about LCC methodology._ It is very difficult to get contractors' data. Companies regard information about their current and future costs—particularly data for predictions and competitive bids—as highly confidential and are unwilling to share it with competitors. Even within DOD it is hard to obtain cost data for past DOD procurements because of intraorganizational factionalism, fear of criticism, simple bureaucratic confusion, or the inherent complexity of multimillion dollar contracts spread over many years with changing requirements. Also, cost-estimating methods vary widely among analysts; there are no commonly accepted costing models.

These problems are characteristic of a new, evolving, growing discipline. In the past, contractors and government agencies have learned that by sharing engineering information with their community they benefit in increased prestige and that their audiences can never quite catch up with them. Similarly, they are learning that the public presentation of cost methods and data gains them increased stature in the industry while their competition must still struggle to emulate them. The problems are being solved step by step by all who work in the field. Data are being compiled in usable forms, old methods are being refined and gaining wider acceptance, and new methods are being developed. As more reports and books are published and as more courses are given, the learning process accelerates, and the accuracy and reliability of estimates improve. Such growing pains are inevitable in a dynamic new field.

5. *Contractors are reluctant to guarantee estimates unless they can control costs.* Critics of LCC doubt that anyone can predict the behavior of a novel, complex man-machine system ten or twenty years in the future. How can the operation and support costs of a new weapon system be estimated before it has been designed? In designing the system, does the contractor have substantial control over military operations and maintenance, which can radically alter the costs? Is it reasonable to ask a contractor to assume a significant financial risk in such a highly uncertain situation?

Many military contractors feel that it is impossible to predict the cost performance of a novel system, particularly the operating and maintenance costs of military personnel. As one small example, Congress and the military services regularly revise personnel policies that contribute to the turnover (reenlistment) rate of uniformed personnel. This turnover rate determines annual training costs and significantly affects personnel skill levels and capabilities. No contractor (nor anyone else for that matter) can predict how these costs will cumulate over a number of years.

In such an environment, many contractors feel that it would be foolhardy to subject their company to possible financial penalties for failing to stay within predicted costs unless the company can prevent such a rise in costs. They think that speculation on cost trade-offs may be an interesting exercise for some systems engineers or logisticians but that companies should not have to sign firm contractual clauses with penalties.

The use of LCC does not require the prediction of the future. Of course, external events may force changes in plans and estimates. A rise in the price of oil or nuclear fuel, a new military threat, or a change in the U.S. military recruitment policies—all can affect plans for a particular weapon or system. LCC estimates are based on a group of assumptions about the future, however, and lose effect if those assumptions cease to be valid. Furthermore, most LCC work involves the comparison of competing systems; anticipated ultimate costs are less important than the assessment of comparative costs of alternative approaches to a problem. Moreover, future changes that diverge from LCC assumptions are likely to affect rival systems equally and are unlikely to reverse the conclusions of an LCC study. In many systems, the investment of an additional dollar in development, testing, or quality control would save many dollars in fuel or maintenance cost. In evaluating such options, errors of a few percent in cost estimates are usually not significant.

There are also contractual solutions to the problem of risk. Various provisions exclude or limit the contractor's liability for cost increases due to unpredictable exogenous events but require him to bear a fair share of the costs arising from program situations and oblige him to control those costs that are within his purview. As will be shown in Chapter 7, there are now procedures to synchronize the contractor's obligations with the development of the system so as to offer a more equitable division of risk between buyer and seller than was available in the past.

The use of LCC has been increasing as these impediments are being solved. The next question is, how is it done?

An Overview of LCC Analysis

The life cycle cost of an item—its total cost at the end of its lifetime—includes all expenses for research and development, production, modification, transportation, introduction of the item into inventory, new facilities, operation, support, maintenance, disposal, and any other costs of ownership, less any salvage revenue at the end of its lifetime (see Figure 1-2)[8] Thus, LCC excludes any costs incurred if the item was not procured, any money that has already been obligated or spent at the time of LCC analysis, and invariant expenses, such as headquarters costs. Costs are estimated on the basis of the existing institutional situation; they do not reflect policy changes that might be desirable in such areas as a more efficient use of manpower or equipment. (An estimate should note that such changes might lower expected costs.) The military services figure LCC on a peacetime basis; they do not try to calculate potential combat losses and replacement problems for LCC purposes.

The life cycle of a system is conveniently divided into phases. The most common practice uses the *research and development* phase, the *production* phase, the *operating and support* phase, and the *disposal* phase. Various other divisions and names are used; for example, the research and development phase may be further divided into the conceptual development phase, the validation phase, and the full-scale development phase; the production phase may be called the investment phase; the operating and support phase may be divided into the deployment phase and the operations phase. Some shifts in meaning are possible; the investment phase may include both production costs and the initial deployment costs. Each of the phases is described in the chapter on estimating that phase; variations from these are possible to

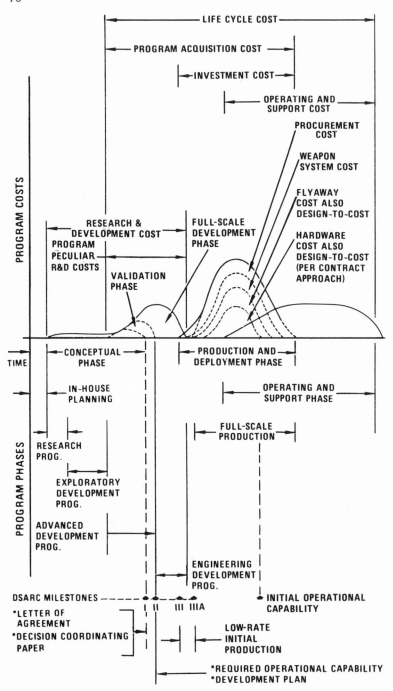

Figure 1-2. Life Cycle of a Materiel System

suit particular agencies or programs, but a clear definition and consistency are mandatory.

Use of LCC

LCC has six primary uses. Some are more relevant to government procurement personnel, and others apply more to contractors; but all share a common methodology. The six uses are:

1. *Long-range planning and budgeting.* At the most basic level, LCC is a method of stimulating orderly planning. An LCC estimate reveals possible alternatives and provides a quantitative discipline for evaluating them. The need to derive money values for an LCC estimate forces management to clarify a maintenance concept or a program operation. Successive estimates provide progressively more details for planning purposes and a quantitative basis for the total budget.

2. *Comparison of competing programs.* LCC analysis makes it possible to compare the costs of a number of alternative ways of meeting an operational requirement.

3. *Comparison of logistics concepts.* The comparative cost of various approaches to the logistic support of a system should be evaluated for the entire life cycle, not just for a particular operation. The sometimes parochial view of, say, the supply organization can be evaluated on the basis of money values—how much each proposed plan costs.

4. *Decisions about the replacement of aging equipment.* Often, intuitive judgments are not borne out by a quantitative analysis. Many operational personnel are swayed either by their attachment to a familiar piece of equipment or by their fascination with the exotic technology of new equipment. A cost analysis helps to separate emotion and facts.

5. *Control over an ongoing program.* As a program progresses and various decisions must be made that involve more than one phase of the life cycle, LCC should be used as a

decision criterion. Therefore the periodic evaluation of the total LCC of the program provides management with a picture of how well these decisions are being made.

No contractual methods of controlling to a specific value of LCC have been developed that are usable early in the life cycle, though methods of controlling large parts of LCC are being used. These include *design to cost, reliability improvement warranty,* and others that progressively place tighter cost controls on the contractor as the life cycle progresses. The most widely used contractual device—design to cost— usually controls the recurring production cost and may be called "design to unit production cost" (DTUPC). One objective of this book is to show how DTUPC may be enlarged to become design to life cycle cost and become part of the overall process of life cycle cost procurement.

6. *Selection among competing contractors.* The most frequent use of LCC has been as the criterion for the selection of a contractor to develop and produce military equipment. Before this is done, positive answers to several questions are necessary. Can explicit performance requirements be written? Will the life of the product be long enough to make operating and support costs a significant part of the total cost? Are enough historical data available to permit a reasonable analysis of LCC? (Some liberties may be taken with this requirement, as the chapters on estimating will discuss.) Is the additional time required for LCC analysis acceptable? Do both the buyer and the seller have the management resources to carry out the LCC analysis?

For each of these applications of LCC, a plan is necessary.

LCC Planning

The plan for an LCC analysis should include the following information:

1. *On what ground rules and assumptions should analysis be based?* All LCC estimates should be based on a set of

ground rules and assumptions that is as specific as possible at the outset of analysis. Revisions may be made in the course of the estimating process.

2. *Which estimating procedures will be used?* The analyst must also decide what forms to use (for example, Figures 1-3 and 1-4), what degree of accuracy and level of detail are required, which data sources to use and their origin (the customer's or the contractor's), how to handle inflation factors, discounting, and other mechanics of the estimating process.

3. *What kind of product is the LCC analysis to produce, for whom, in what format, for what purpose?* (Are the estimates for management controls or for working-level analysis?)

4. *On what schedule will the LCC analysis be carried out?* When will it begin? When will data be obtained? When are estimates due? When will the analysis be complete? A manpower loading chart should be included to show the effort to be devoted to the task.

5. *How will the buyer's and seller's managements audit and control the LCC process?* How frequent will reviews be? Will they be oral or written, delivered or filed?

6. *How will the LCC effort be organized and financed?* What individuals or groups are to perform which tasks, and how are funds to be allocated among them? How will the LCC work be integrated with the tasks of design, planning, and control?

Timing

Regardless of whether LCC analysis is being used for internal planning procedures or in a competition among contractors, some general principles of timing apply. First, LCC analysis should start as early as possible in the consideration of a product or system, preferably during the conceptual phase. At that point, a very rough order-of-magnitude estimate

ROW	PRIME APPRO	DEFN REF	COST ELEMENT (SYSTEM STRUCTURE)	(1) FRAME	(2) PROPULSION	(3) GUIDANCE CONTROL COMMUNICATIONS	(9) COMMON SUPPORT EQUIPMENT	(10) OTHER	(11) TOTAL	(12) PERCENT
1		1.0	RESEARCH AND DEVELOPMENT			*THE COLUMN HEADINGS SHOWN ARE GENERIC, USED FOR DISCUSSION OF SYSTEMS IN GENERAL. FOR SPECIFIC STUDY, SPECIFIC COLUMN HEADINGS ARE THOSE PROVIDED IN APPENDIX A.				
2	RDTE	1.01	DEVELOPMENT ENGINEERING							
3	RDTE	1.02	PRODUCIBILITY ENGINEERING AND PLANNING (PEP)							
4	RDTE	1.03	TOOLING							
5	RDTE	1.04	PROTOTYPE MANUFACTURING							
6	RDTE	1.05	DATA							
7	RDTE	1.06	SYSTEM TEST AND EVALUATION							
8	RD OM	1.07	SYSTEM PROJECT MANAGEMENT							
9	RD OM	1.08	TRAINING							
10	RD MC	1.09	FACILITIES							
11	RDTE	1.10	OTHER							
12		2.0	INVESTMENT							
13	PR MC	2.01	NON RECURRING INVESTMENT							
14	PROC	2.02	PRODUCTION							
15	PROC	2.03	ENGINEERING CHANGES							
32	OMA	3.022	PETROLEUM OIL AND LUBRICANTS							
33	PROC	3.023	UNIT TRAINING AMMUNITION AND MISSILES							
34		3.03	DEPOT MAINTENANCE							
35	OMA	3.031	LABOR							
36	PR OM	3.032	MATERIEL							
37	OMA	3.033	TRANSPORTATION							
38	PROC	3.04	MODIFICATIONS MATERIEL							
39		3.05	OTHER DIRECT SUPPORT OPERATIONS							
40	OMA	3.051	MAINTENANCE CIVILIAN LABOR							
41	OMA	3.052	OTHER DIRECT							
42		3.06	INDIRECT SUPPORT OPERATIONS							
43	MP OM	3.061	PERSONNEL REPLACEMENT							
44	MPA	3.062	TRANSIENTS PATIENTS AND PRISONERS							
45	OMA	3.063	QUARTERS MAINTENANCE AND UTILITIES							
46	MP OM	3.064	MEDICAL SUPPORT							
47	OMA	3.065	OTHER INDIRECT			S. U.S. ARMY, "STANDARDS FOR PRESENTATION AND DOCUMENTATION OF LIFE CYCLE COST ESTIMATES", PAMPHLET 11-5, MAY 1976.				
48			TOTAL SYSTEM COST (LESS ERDA)							
49	ERDA	4.0	ERDA COST							
50			TOTAL SYSTEM COST (WITH ERDA)							

Figure 1-3. Army Life Cycle Cost Reporting Format

COST DATA AND VARIABLE EXPLANATION SHEET

PROGRAM PHASE _____ DEFN REF & ROW NO. _____ PRIME APPRO. ____
COST ELEMENT _____ WBS _____

FY 19 ____	COST-ESTIMATING RELATION AND LIMITATIONS	VARIABLE VALUES USED
FY 19 ____		
FY 19 ____		
FY 19 ____		
FY 19 ____		
FY 19 ____		
FY 19 ____		
FY 19 ____		
FY 19 ____		
FY 19 ____		
FY 19 ____		
FY 19 ____		
FY 19 ____		
FY 19 ____		
TOTAL ____	RATIONALE FOR INPUTS, C.E.R. OR OTHER COST-ESTIMATING METHOD	

CALCULATIONS AND REFERENCES:

Figure 1-4. Cost Data and Variable Explanation Sheet

may show whether the program will or will not fit into a budget of, say, $1.8 billion. For example, calculations might show that the concept for a new tank calls for one that is 20 percent heavier and 20 percent more complex than its predecessor, so that its procurement cost would be about 40 percent higher than the old one. If the old tanks cost $1 million each, then the new tank might be estimated at $1.4 million each, or $700 million for 500 tanks. The development costs might be estimated in a similar way to be $50 million. Operating and support costs might be estimated on the basis of a crew of three at a cost of about $50,000 per man per year, or $900 million for three men in 500 tanks for twelve years. The sum of the estimates of the three phases is $1.65 billion, just within the $1.8 billion limit. By starting the LCC analysis at the conceptual phase, it is still possible to ask whether it would be wiser to produce a new tank or to modify the old one. Note that the LCC estimate for the existing tank starts with any necessary refurbishment costs, *not* at its original procurement cost. Differences in operation and support costs for the two tanks (skill levels of the crew, reliability of the tank, maintenance requirements, fuel consumption) might favor either the production of the new tank or the modernization of the old one.

Second, as the program progresses, more and more detailed estimates can be made of the LCC, using more and more precise methods (see Figure 1-5). The analyst should recognize the appropriate estimating tool for the particular phase of the program. As later chapters show, the three methods of estimating—analogy, parametric, and the industrial engineering approach—provide increasing accuracy and depth of analysis for additional effort.

Estimates by analogy are based on a similar past program or task, with adjustments for differences in the present program; if possible, more than one past program is used. If data on many programs are available, a generalized relationship may be developed between some program character-

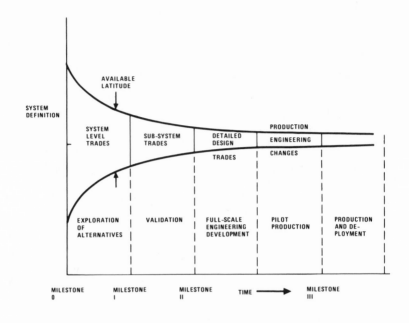

COST DEFINITION	AFFORDABILITY RANGE	LCC ELEMENTS GOALS & THRESHOLD	FIRM DTC REQUIREMENTS & O & S TARGETS	FIRM PRODUCTION AND O & S REQUIREMENTS
PERFORMANCE DEFINITION	MISSION NEEDS	PERFORMANCE GOALS & THRESHOLDS & OPERATIONAL CON-CEPTS	FIRM PERFORMANCE REQUIREMENTS AND LOGISTICS PLANS	DETAILED DESIGN DATA AND LOGISTICS METHODS

AFTER A CHART BY CDR. SCOTT MOBLEY, USN

Figure 1-5.   Balancing Cost and Performance
During System Development

istic(s) and the cost. Such "parametric" relationships are called "Cost Estimating Relations" (CERs) and are usually equations that include one to three characteristics of the program. Both estimates by analogy and parametric methods are "top down" methods, because they examine the program as a whole. The older, industrial engineering method is a "bottom up" technique that develops detail costs for each of the parts that make up the whole program. Because the people who will do the work often provide the estimates, the industrial engineering method is also called the "grass roots" approach.

Table 1-1

DISCIPLINES REQUIRED FOR LIFE CYCLE COSTING

Accounting	Computer Science
Contracting	Engineering
Estimating	Finance
Logistics	Maintainability
Management	Manufacturing Engineering
Quality Control	Reliability
Statistical Analysis	

LCC Organization

The group that plans, calculates, and presents the LCC estimate makes LCC work. It must have close ties to the cadres
in financial estimating, budgeting and accounting, logistics
planning, design, testing, and, of course, management. Several
organizational arrangements have been used to integrate the
LCC staff with these departments. In most cases, the LCC
group is part of either the logistics department or the financial analysis department. Close coordination with logistics is
desirable because so much of LCC is operating and support
cost; close coordination with the financial analysis department is desirable because LCC is, finally, a financial and
estimating effort. The DOD has placed most of its LCC
analysis organizations with cost analysis groups and has
found this solution satisfactory; many contractors have done
the same thing.

LCC analysts require skills in many disciplines (see Table 1-1). Because individual analysts rarely have all these skills, they must call on other specialists, usually from some other group, for a completely self-contained LCC group is unnecessarily expensive. Furthermore, the necessity to work with other groups promotes a desirable involvement in LCC by other parts of the organization. The real work of LCC is then done by those who determine LCC—the designers, the planners, the test engineers, the tooling engineers, and the logisticians, under the guidance and monitoring of LCC analysts.

Cost Drivers

The LCC effort has been characterized as the search for those product characteristics that result in large support costs; this presupposes that support costs are the major cost drivers (and they usually are). Stated more broadly, LCC is the search for the significant costs that can be influenced by planning and design decisions. Therefore a major task of LCC analysis is to discover and illuminate such cost drivers. These factors may be as broad as the number and type of targets or crew pay and allowances, or as narrow as the environmental vibration frequency requirements or the system reaction time. When these are recognized, concerted efforts can be applied to reduce the few cost drivers and the total LCC.

Summary

1. Procurement based on minimizing LCC can significantly reduce the government's total budget.

2. Early resistances to LCC are being overcome.

3. LCC can be used for planning and budgeting decisions involving competitive approaches and the control of programs.

4. If a procurement is to be based on LCC: (a) performance requirements should be written, not oral; (b) oper-

ating and support costs should be a significant part of the total cost; (c) historical cost data should be available; (d) time to do the analysis should be available; (e) buyer and seller management should have the capability to use LCC.

5. An LCC plan provides necessary guidance for the task of analysis.

6. Start LCC as early as possible in the program, when it can be most beneficial.

7. The LCC group should be part of the logistics or the financial organization.

8. The discovery and reduction of cost drivers provide an economical means of controlling costs.

Notes

1. The Department of Defense budget considers all personnel costs as part of "operation and support."

2. U.S. Executive Office of the President, Office of Management and Budget, *Major Systems Acquisition*, Circular No. A-109, April 5, 1976, U.S. Executive Office of the President, Office of Management and Budget, Office of Federal Procurement Policy, *Major Systems Acquisition, A Discussion of the Application of OMB Circular No. A-109*, Pamphlet no. 1, August 1976; U.S. Department of Defense, *Design to Cost*, Directive no. 5000.28 (Washington, D.C.: Department of Defense, 1975); U.S. Department of Defense, Joint Logistics Commanders' Guide to Design-to-Cost, *Life Cycle Cost as a Design Parameter*, DARCOM P700-6, NAVMAT P5242, AFLCP/AFSCP 800-19 (Washington, D.C.: Department of Defense, 1977).

3. U.S. Congress, House, *Department of Defense Appropriations Bill*, 94th Cong., 1st sess., 1975, October 1, 1975, pp. 9387-9407.

4. R. C. Buyse and J. H. Taylor, *Return on Assets and Risk Analysis Using Life Cycle Cost Techniques* (St. Peters-

burg, Fla.: Honeywell, 1977); and Reynolds, Smith, and Hills, Architects-Engineers-Planners, Inc., *Life Cycle Costing Emphasizing Energy Conservation: Guidelines for Investment Analysis* (Jacksonville, Fla.: Reynolds, Smith, and Hills, 1977).

·5. U.S. Congress, Senate, Committee on Government Operations, *Report of the Commission on Government Procurement, Part C, Acquisition of Major Systems,* vol. 2, 94th Cong., 1st sess., 1975, p. 83.

6. U.S. Congress, House, *Department of Defense Appropriations Bill,* 94th Cong., 1st sess., 1975, p. 9387.

7. U.S. Congress, Senate, *Report on Government Procurement,* p. 129.

8. Although the formal definition includes all research and development costs as part of LCC, Figure 1-2 omits the research and exploratory development costs. If LCC can be estimated prior to the exploratory development, then all anticipated costs should be included. If LCC is estimated at any later time, all previous costs are considered "sunk" costs and are not included in the total LCC as of that time. In any case, the research and exploratory development costs are usually a very small part of LCC.

2
Research and Development Costs

This chapter, and the next three, will discuss the methods of estimating costs. The LCC analyst will usually depend on estimating specialists; most organizations conducting LCC analyses will have one or more departments designated to provide engineering, production, and support cost estimates. These organizations should be used whenever possible, and the analyst must be familiar with their terminology, methods, strengths, and weaknesses. Occasionally, because of the short time available or the paucity of information, the analyst may attempt to develop approximate cost estimates himself. The following chapters will provide the background needed to use the estimating organization and to develop rough, order-of-magnitude estimates.

Research and development (R&D) costs include all of the expenses necessary to produce a set of engineering drawings and specifications for release to manufacturing; this covers the conceptual, validation, and full-scale development phases. It also includes systems engineering studies, design, development, testing, prototype fabrication and testing, pilot line fabrication, operations and support planning, and manufacturing planning. Also covered are customer testing, such as technical and operational evaluation, qualification tests, but not service tests or production acceptance tests. During the

R&D phase, the initial logistics plans will be drawn up, with ideas for maintenance, training, provisioning, support equipment, facilities, and others. There are significant costs during R&D for both the contractor and the customer; both types of costs should be fully developed and coordinated. Either the contractor's or the customer's analyst can easily overlook significant expenses in the other's house.

Order-of-Magnitude Estimates

The first approach to R&D costs should be a rough, order-of-magnitude estimate based on general experience or intuition. Does this task require one man, ten men, or one thousand men? Will it take a week or three years? Is there an elaborate test program, with expensive facilities? The very first estimate might be in such gross terms as "fifteen men at the contractor and five in the customer program office, which costs out to $1.2 million." In this example, a man-year, with the supporting supervision, material, travel, computer time, and so forth, approximates $60,000; for a first estimate, that is enough detail. Later the estimate will be refined. A more satisfactory order-of-magnitude estimate might be made on the basis of a specific analogy, that is, similarity to a previous program, which cost $1.5 million. Let us say that the new program under consideration is to be only two-thirds as large but requires a more difficult schedule. If a tight schedule is thought to increase the costs by, say, 25 percent, the estimate would now be $1.5 million x 2/3 x 1.25 = $1.25 million. Gratifyingly close! This answer should be considered the same as the previous estimate; the $50,000 difference is not significant. If the contractor or customer remains interested upon learning that the program will cost on the order of $1.2 million for R&D, then more detailed calculations should be made.

Three Basic Methods of Estimating

Each of the three basic methods of estimating is effective for research and development costs. Analogy is the easiest and is usually used early in the program, as was seen in the discussion of order-of-magnitude estimates. If more information and preparatory work are available, parametric methods (CERs) can be used. Later in the program, when detailed, specific tasks are known and increased accuracy is desired, and it is worth spending the time and money to develop such estimates, an industrial engineering estimate should be developed using the engineers who will do the development tasks. These three methods are used to estimate R&D costs, production costs, operating and support costs, and miscellaneous costs (see also Chapters 3, 4, and 5).

Analogy to Other Programs

The method of analogy was used in the above example relating the cost of a current program to that of a previous one. This method may be used for the R&D program as a whole, as in the above example, or for parts of the program. Second, the modification to the analogous program may be applied to one or more factors, e.g., complexity, schedule, advancement in the state of the art, customer involvement, data and prototype deliveries, and so on. The accuracy of the method depends, of course, on the ability of the analyst to perceive the similarities and differences between programs. If parts of the program are to be estimated separately, such divisions as systems analysis, testing, design, prototype fabrication, and material requirements should be considered. Separate judgments then compare each part of the new program with an analogous program. For example, the systems analysis task of the new program of airborne electronic equipment might be judged equal to that of the old, with

Table 2-1
COST ESTIMATE BY ANALOGY
(in millions of $)

Cost Element	Base Program Model 10	New Program Model Z
Systems engineering and program management	2.0	2.2 (a)
Design	8.0	11.2 (b)
Prototype fabrication and material	1.5	1.1 (c)
Flight and laboratory test	3.0	1.5 (d)
Total	14.5	16.0

Notes:

(a) Systems engineering and program management for Model Z are similar to those of Model 10; the 10% increase in Model Z is due to larger task of design monitoring.

(b) In Model Z, the additional design task of the moving target indicator adds 20%, and higher performance requirements will require another 20%, for a total of 140% of the cost of Model 10.

(c) Model Z requires only two prototypes versus three for Model 10; tooling and other fixed costs were about $300,000 for Model 10, with each prototype at $400,000.

(d) Model Z requires only 1 aircraft model qualification; flight test personnel estimate the cost at one-half that of Model 10.

somewhat greater program management effort; the design task might be 40 percent larger because of a new moving target indicator and higher performance requirements. On the other hand, the new program may include a flight test in only one type of aircraft, whereas the previous program had to be tested in three aircraft; the new flight test costs might be halved for this reason. Such an example is shown in Table 2-1.

Estimates by analogy can usually be done fairly easily and quickly. More important, management finds them appealing and easy to understand. Such estimates are usually surprisingly accurate if all the significant changes between the two programs are understood and properly accounted for. If one prepares such an estimate by analogy to two programs, the similarity of results can be very reassuring. This is especially true if the two previous programs are of different types and if one is larger and the other smaller than the instant program.

In order to use the analogy method, good records must be kept. Analysts should develop files in the fields that they are likely to have to estimate; the estimating organization may be the repository for these files. Of course, the next estimate required will always be in an area for which analogous history is not on file, and the estimator will have to search for data.

Parametric Methods: Cost-Estimating Relations

These methods assume that one or more parameters of the program explain the cost. For example, in preparing the rough, order-of-magnitude estimate above, a simple parametric relation was used—the number of men working on the project is proportional to the cost. More precisely, this may be expressed in mathematical form as:

$$\text{Development cost} = (\text{number of men}) \times (\text{years worked}) \times (\text{cost constant per man-year})$$

In the example, $60,000 per man-year was suggested as the cost constant as an approximation of the total cost of salary, overhead, material, travel, computers, and so on. The use of this equation, or cost-estimating relation (CER), requires a knowledge of the manpower required for the development project. The CER transforms the problem from one of estimating dollars to one of estimating a more familiar and more accessible variable—the number of people at work. Some

Table 2-2
R&D COST ESTIMATING
RELATIONS IN VARIOUS FIELDS
(in 1978 dollars)

Development Engineering Manpower Cost = \$60,000 x (number of man-years)
System Test and Evaluation = (cost per test period) x (number of test periods)
Contractor Management Costs = $\sum_{i=1}^{i=k}$ (contractor management costs for the __ i __ year) where k = total number of project years
Software Development Costs = 3 (cost per man-month) x (number of assembly- level instructions)/(difficulty constant)

where the Difficulty Constant is if the Program is

Difficulty Constant	Program
500	Easy
250	Medium
100	Hard

Total software development cost includes the total cost of design, program, implement, test and document, with overhead costs such as secretarial, management, and the like.
In the construction industry — Architectural and Engineering Costs = 10 percent of construction costs
The percentage is higher for projects over \$500,000, and lower for projects under \$500,000, and lower for significantly larger projects; higher for complex plants such as chemical and power plants; lower for office buildings and homes.
Missile Airframe Development Costs = \$810,000 + 24,000 x (total missile weight in pounds) for tactical missiles less than 200 pounds.

CERs that are useful in research and development are given in Table 2-2. They were developed by a number of organizations from their own experience. They are typical of CERs used in various fields and may be taken as examples for the development of new estimating relations. Note particularly the estimating relation used in the construction industry, where architectural and engineering costs are estimated as a fraction of total construction costs. This kind of estimating technique is sometimes called cost-cost estimating.

A more sophisticated CER assumes that the development cost of an equipment varies in accordance with the physical or performance parameters of that equipment. For example, the development cost may be thought to vary as a function of the weight of a radar, or perhaps as a function of the power output of that radar. Expressed as equations, these would be:

$$\text{Development Cost} = k \, (\text{weight})^x \qquad\qquad 2\text{-}1$$

$$\text{Development Cost} = q \, (\text{power})^z \qquad\qquad 2\text{-}2$$

Using the known cost of a number of previously developed radars, plot on one sheet of log-log graph paper the development cost for each against the weight and use another sheet to plot the cost against power as in Figures 2-1 and 2-2.[1] Note that power seems to explain the cost variations of the different radars more satisfactorily than weight. Therefore we should use equation 2-2 as the CER. A straight "average" line drawn through the points yields the slope, which equals z, and the value of q may then be calculated from the data for any point on the line. The set of data should be from as coherent a group as possible. All radars should be of the same type: all shipboard, search radars of approximately the same frequency, the same display and computational ability, range, and so on. Rarely is it possible to gather a set of data that meets all these criteria; roughly similar data are used, and the scatter in the data is often attributed to these disparities.

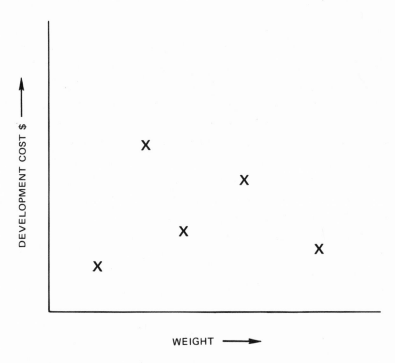

Figure 2-1. Radar CER Based on Weight

The "average" curve can be drawn by eye as a best approximation. There are a number of more precise methods of
deriving such curves, however. Other forms for CERs can be
power equations and combinations of straight-line segments.

In the case of a straight-line (linear) cost-estimating relation, a "least squares" approximation can be done quickly
and easily. This analytical method derives from the theory
that the best straight line is the one with the least variance
from the points to the line. In other words, the sum of the
squares of the distance from the points to the line is mini-
mized. The procedure may be found in any introductory
applied statistics text.[2] There are computer programs to do
the task.

If the underlying relationship is believed to be a curve,
more elaborate methods, such as curvilinear regression, can

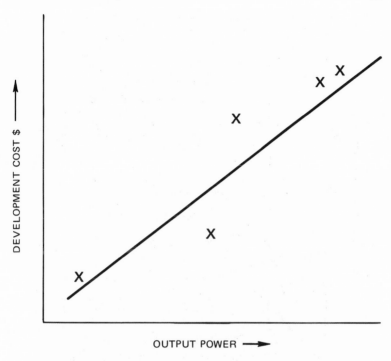

Figure 2-2.   Radar C ER Based on Output Power

be used. Methods are also available to analyze the effects of more than one variable, for example, if both weight and power were used as the parameters to explain the cost of the radar. These methods are known as "multiple correlation" procedures and can separate the effect on cost of each of the independent parameters. Statistics texts provide these methods, and computer programs are available to do the tiresome arithmetic. The ease of using computers, however, should not tempt one to analyze the data beyond their worth. The scatter in the data may be truly random and not indicative of another significant parameter. Try to distinguish between functional relations and random variations.

The CERs can be developed for each of various kinds of radars or other equipments; families of CERs can be developed for airborne radars, ground radars, and mobile radars.

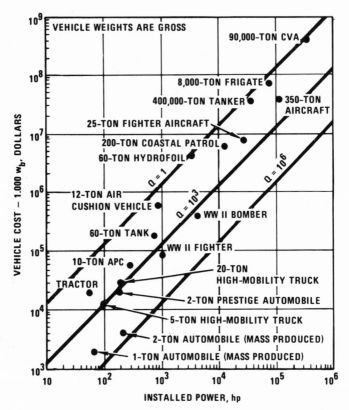

Figure 2-3. Vehicle Cost in Terms of Installed
Power, Empty Weight, and Number Built

The CERs can be elaborated to evaluate the effects of frequency change, range, environments, and the like. Unfortunately, the cost of developing such CERs usually discourages
such efforts. Therefore, in practice, CERs are usually restricted to no more than two variables, with perhaps an additional factor or two, which add fixed amounts of cost.

Dix and Riddell provide excellent, comprehensive CERs
for quick estimates in an unfamiliar field.[3] Figure 2-3 is an
example of the material available. A more precise parametric
estimating method, called Programmed Review of Information for Costing and Evaluation (PRICE), has been developed
by RCA. The PRICE computer program is particularly valu-

able for estimating engineering development costs of electronic equipment (it can also provide manufacturing cost estimates and operating and support cost estimates). It does not use the performance characteristics of the equipment. Rather, it uses the physical characteristics, such as weight, volume, manufacturing complexity, schedules, power input, and so forth, as input data. The PRICE computer program contains a large number of CERs, which together develop cost estimates. This model has been highly successful for many defense applications and routinely provides estimates to accuracies of plus or minus 10 percent. Its accuracy seems to be a function of the skill of the analyst, as with most other methods.

Even the best parametric methods, such as PRICE, are standardized for a particular engineering and development organization. It is possible to use CERs developed by others, but do so with caution. All of the terms and conditions should be studied and made applicable to the situation under consideration. For example, test costs may be part of the engineering department's responsibility in one organization and of the manufacturing department's in another. The CERs for one organization must be calibrated for use elsewhere.

CERs are developed from data for a limited range of each variable. As with all descriptions of physical phenomena, the CER should be used with caution outside of that range. For example, if the weights of the radars considered in developing the CER range from 100 to 1,200 pounds, it may not be possible accurately to predict the cost of a proposed radar of 2,000 pounds; any estimate of the cost of 20,000-pound radar would almost certainly be highly inaccurate.

Grass Roots Estimate: Industrial Engineering Method

The most acceptable and time-honored approach to engineering cost estimates is to ask the people who will have to do the job how much it will cost. They certainly ought to know and they do. That is, they do if they receive the proper directions. They must have a clear description of the task (a statement of work with performance specifications, data requirements, test requirements, and so on), a definition of which organization does each task, and a schedule. Each part of the organization is then requested to estimate the cost of doing the task assigned to it. It does this estimating generally by analogy, by its own CERs, or by even more esoteric methods. The sum of these estimates represents the total cost of the program. The cost analyst must see to it that all tasks are estimated once and only once; the objective is a complete estimate with no omissions or duplications. It is often a good idea to send a preliminary statement of work and a schedule to the operational people for their comment before sending them the formal request for estimate. The use of a form for the submission of cost estimates facilitates the job of the estimators and simplifies the input of the data to a computer. Figure 2-4 is an example of such a form.

Some words of caution are in order. If the estimators understand that their figures are to be the basis for future budgets, they are likely to inflate their estimates to provide a cushion for future problems. Knowing that the cost analyst anticipates such inflation and will pare the estimate on this basis, the estimator may try to inflate the estimate even more. The result can be disastrous. The problem can be reduced if meaningful target estimates are established in advance and distributed with the request for estimate. Deviations from these targets require explanation. Alternatively, the estimators can suggest changes in the task description or schedule that will enable them to meet the target. The solution is to have a competent and trusted cost analyst present the request in a responsible manner. Any changes in the estimate should be discussed with the originator, whose concurrence should be obtained. In discussing the estimate with its originator, the analyst might use the previously discussed estimating methods. How much did similar tasks cost in the

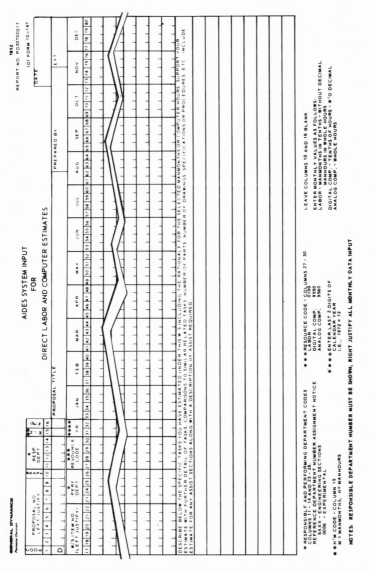

Figure 2-4. Estimating Computer Input Form

past? How does this job differ from the previous job, expressed quantitatively? How can this problem be solved more economically than before? Through such a reasoned discussion, a mutual agreement can be reached on an estimate.

One significant advantage of the grass roots estimate is that it clarifies the cost of detail requirements. Neither the analogy nor the parametric method makes the cost of particular details visible. If the program cost is estimated on the basis of the number of man-years, it is not possible, for example, to see the effect of a change in the use of computers or of more detail-level testing. Grass roots estimates, by shedding light on such important areas, help program management decisions. Moreover, though each estimate may have a large error, the summation of many estimates tends to cancel such errors (if they are random, not systematic). There are many other aspects to estimating, including overhead costs and profit, to name the most important. In the next chapter, these and other refinements of the three estimating methods will be discussed.

Work Breakdown Structure

The detail cost estimate should be organized in a systematic fashion to ensure that all elements of work are covered. The framework for this is a work breakdown structure (WBS). Similar and related concepts are the cost breakdown structure and the hardware breakdown structure (see below).

The Department of Defense has a standard, MIL-STD-881, which defines and describes the WBS to be used for various military programs.[4] The standard awkwardly (for LCC purposes) defines a WBS as "a product oriented family tree composed of hardware, services, and data which result from project engineering efforts during the development and production of a defense material item, and which completely defines the project program. A WBS displays and defines the product(s) to be developed or produced and relates the elements of work to be accomplished to each other and to the end product." Sample WBSs for aircraft, ships, missiles, electronics, and the like are provided in the standard. The missile system WBS (Table 2-3) is typical. Note that at level two, only the first two items are operational hardware. Thus, the scope of the WBS, (and of the LCC) extends beyond operational hardware and its development and production. Each of the categories must be costed, thereby capturing all assignable costs of the system. The WBS contains far more than the R&D costing.

Note that the WBS is not an organizational structure; it does not show organizational supremacy. Note also that it is not an assembly sequence diagram; it does not show manufacturing methods. Moreover, it may not show the hardware functional relationships; disparate elements are often placed in close juxtaposition. In practice, however, the WBS is constructed to reflect all of these, insofar as conflicts among them can be resolved.

The military WBS is intended to gather costs for the entire program life cycle. During the R&D phase, only three or four of the level-two categories may be pertinent. For example, the hardware items require much development effort, but the training category may be empty of costs. Certainly very little money is spent on "operational site activation" during the R&D phase. Therefore some of the elements of the WBS may not be used during R&D. The WBS will grow and emphasis will change during the various phases of the program as more of the categories are used and details are added at lower levels.

Variability and Risk

The estimating process itself has an uncertainty, or variability, which is defined as cost risk. Assuming that the statement of work is correct, cost risk is the possible variation in actual costs; this variation may be due to errors in the

Table 2-3
SUMMARY WORK BREAKDOWN STRUCTURE

Level 1	Level 2	Level 3
Missile System	Air Vehicle	Integration and Assembly
		Propulsion (For Single Stage Only)
		Stage I
		Stage II
		Stage III
		Stage IV
		Guidance and Control Equipment Launched Payload
		Payload Shroud
		Airborne Test Equipment
		Airborne Training Equipment
		Auxiliary Equipment
	Command and Launch Equipment	Integration and Assembly Surveillance, Identification, and Tracking Sensors
		Launch and Guidance Control
		Communications
		Data Processing
		Launcher Equipment
		Auxiliary Equipment
	Training	Equipment
		Services
		Facilities
	Peculiar Support Equipment	Organizational/Intermediate (Including Equipment Common to Depot)
		Depot (Only)

Table 2-3. SUMMARY WORK BREAKDOWN
STRUCTURE (Continued)

Level 1	Level 2	Level 3
	Systems Test and Evaluation	Development Test and Evaluation
		Operational Test and Evaluation
		Mockups
		Test and Evaluation Support
		Test Facilities
	Systems/Project Management	Systems Engineering
		Project Management
	Data	Technical Publications
		Engineering Data
		Management Data
		Support Data
		Data Depository
	Operational/ Site Activation	Contractor Technical Support
		Site Construction
		Site/Ship/Vehicle Conversion
		System Assembly, Installation, and Checkout on Site
	Common Support Equipment	Organizational/Intermediate (Including Equipment Common to Depot)
		Depot (Only)
	Industrial Facilities	Construction/Conversion/Expansion
		Equipment Acquisition or Modernization
		Maintenance
	Initial Spares and Initial Repair Parts	(Specify by allowance list, grouping, of hardware element)

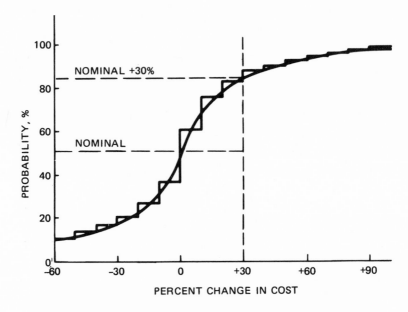

Figure 2-5.   Cumulative Cost-Risk Function

methods used, or it may be due to unknowable future events, such as a change in management personnel. This suggests a probability distribution of the variation of the actual costs from the estimate. The cost risk is regarded as separate from technical risk and schedule risk, even though both of these have significant effects on costs.

In the case of cost risk, the objective is to convey information to decision makers in an effective manner. The use of a point estimate or single number does not reflect the uncertainty associated with the estimate and also implies a precise value. One way of reflecting the uncertainty is to provide a range of costs; this range might reflect the plus or minus 90 percent or plus or minus 95 percent confidence intervals. A more precise and mathematically elegant technique is to use a probability distribution function to describe the variation in costs. A probability function, such as the one in Figure 2-5, can show the change in cost plotted against the cumulative probability of that change. General practice is limited to expressing cost risk as the upper and lower bounds to the most likely or mean value; these bounds are the plus or minus 90 percent points.

How are the data obtained for such evaluations? The analyst can attempt to estimate these risk probabilities himself. It is hard to be objective about an estimate one has developed. A good idea is to quantify the risk associated with an estimate by querying various cost and design experts in a structured manner. Questions such as "Is the true value of the costs more likely to lie above or below this value?" can detect any bias in the data. Then, "What is the lowest (or most optimistic) probable cost?" and "What is the highest (or most pessimistic) probable cost?" will determine variability. The answers to these last two questions should be treated as the 90 percent values. Although some authorities suggest determining from the experts the quartile (25 percent and 75 percent) values, these are often more difficult questions for the experts to answer and are not recommended. Incidentally, surveys of this kind will often elicit a great deal of other valuable information for the analyst, e.g., the aspects of the task that are the most costly.

Correction of Bias

Cost estimates tend to be optimistic. Experience rarely shows large underruns of estimates; we have many examples of 100 percent or even 200 percent overruns. (Overruns come with fine explanations; cost savings require only modesty, not discussion.) Here is a simple method to combine estimates to compensate for the optimistic bias. Calculate the average of the experts' expected values, labeling it M. Then let C_o be the average of the experts' optimistic values and C_p be the average of their pessimistic values. The suggested treatment is analogous to the PERT (program review and evaluation technique) method of network analysis. The expected value, C_e, is biased upward, as in equation 2-3.

$$C_e = (C_o + 3M + 2C_p)/6 \qquad\qquad 2\text{-}3$$

That is, a high cost is twice as likely to occur as a low cost, and the most probable cost is weighted three times the low. The reader may wish to bias the estimate of the expected value more or less. Then, as in PERT analysis, the standard deviation is assumed to equal one-sixth of the difference between the high and low estimates, as in equation 2-4.

$$SD = (C_p - C_o)/6 \qquad\qquad 2\text{-}4$$

These values of expected value and standard deviation may then be used to construct distribution curves. The most common distribution is the normal distribution, which is symmetrical and infinite in both directions. The Beta function is a more desirable distribution because it has the features of finiteness over an established range and zero at the end points. The derived expected value and standard deviation may also be used in the Beta distribution.[5]

These procedures make it possible to determine the cost-risk function for a given cost estimate. These distribution functions may then be combined according to the WBS hierarchy to give the cost-risk function at higher levels and the cost-risk function for the total estimate.

Technical Risk

Technical risk is a somewhat more elusive concept than cost risk. The quantitative expression of technical risk is an attempt to state the relative difficulty of the successful development of a new item or project. Such forecasting is one of the more difficult LCC projections. As a general rule, the size of the engineering development program for an item is a measure of the technical risk. Of course, a large new bridge may be an uncomplicated project and require many engineering man-hours, while a new invention attempt may be highly risky and only require a single individual for a few weeks. In the absence of other information, if one program takes twice as many engineering man-months as another, the first has twice the technical problems, and therefore risk, as the second. There may be other influences on the size of the engineering effort; the requirements, the schedule, the documentation, the sheer size of the product—all can change the engineering effort. As a readily available and quantifiable measure, the total engineering manpower is suggested as the measure of technical risk. This measure, unfortunately, is not usually converted into dollars, nor is it expressed as a tolerance or distribution function; the ratio of the risk for two programs can be calculated if a quantitative comparison would be helpful. Rarely, however, is technical risk clear enough to warrant sophisticated analytical measures.

Schedule Risk

Schedule risk is midway between cost risk and technical risk in difficulty. The schedule risk of any given item of a program is fairly easily determined by a poll of expert opinion, as has been suggested for cost risk. Bias may be even more optimistic than for cost risk. Quantification and analysis of schedule risk can be handled in much the same way as for cost risk. In the case of schedule risk, however, it is much more difficult to combine the risk of each item of a program than it is to give the risk of the program as a whole. In theory, if one item of a program is delayed, work on all others could be halted to wait for the laggard to catch up. In practice, it is difficult to detect the delay early enough to take action. Second, the action required is extremely difficult. Halting the effort on other items means diverting manpower and other resources. In a large organization, this is a slow and incomplete process. Therefore the degree of success possible in rescheduling resources when part of the program is delayed is really a measure of the ability of management. Most LCC analysts do not have this measure readily available, nor are they likely to gain universal acceptance for their estimate of management capability. Therefore schedule risk is usually determined only for each individual item and converted to equivalent dollars of cost. The sum of these cost variations will give a simple and optimistic measure of the schedule risk of the entire program. If more sophisticated treatments of risk and uncertainty are desired, Gerald Fleischer has provided a compendium of recent thinking on decision making under uncertainty.[6]

Notes

1. Log-log graph paper has axes marked with the logarithms of the values and is obtainable from engineering stationery suppliers.

2. Irwin Miller and John E. Freund, *Probability and Statistics for Engineers* (Englewood Cliffs, N.J.: Prentice-Hall, 1965); Adam M. Neville and John B. Kennedy, *Basic Statistical Methods for Engineers and Scientists* (Scranton, Pa.: International Textbook, 1964).

3. Donald M. Dix and Fred R. Riddell, "Projecting Cost-Performance Trade-offs for Military Vehicles," *Astronautics and Aeronautics*, September 1976, pp. 40-49.

4. U.S., Department of Defense, *Work Breakdown Structure for Defense Material Items*, MIL-STD-881 (Washington, D.C.: Department of Defense, 1975).

5. Richard Stevens Burrington and Donald Curtis May, Jr., *Handbook of Probability and Statistics with Tables* (New York: McGraw-Hill, 1970).

6. Gerald A. Fleischer, ed., *Risk and Uncertainty: Non-Deterministic Decision Making in Engineering Economy* (Norcross, Ga.: Engineering Economy Division, American Institute of Industrial Engineers, 1975).

3
Production Costs

Production cost estimating is the oldest, most used, and most developed of the cost-estimating procedures. The body of writing on the subject can provide background information.[1] The estimates developed by the production estimating department are usually very good on specific items (poor estimators are eliminated after their overestimates lose contracts or their underestimates produce losses). Frequently, however, the estimates may be too limited in scope for LCC purposes, and the analyst must be aware of the exclusions. For example, contractor estimators often overlook customer costs; government estimators often forget some of the contractor's expenses. The following discussion provides a general background for the evaluation of production cost estimates to be used in life cycle costing.

Production costs are incurred during the production phase, the second of the life cycle phases. The production phase is often considered to include the initial customer costs, such as personnel training, testing, transportation, and facilities. Some agencies then call this the *investment* phase.

Manufacturing Planning

In order to estimate manufacturing costs, a description or

plan of the job is needed. The precision of an estimate depends, as noted before, on the purpose of the estimate and the resources devoted to its preparation. Rough, order-of-magnitude estimates can be developed inexpensively with a very brief, preliminary manufacturing plan that may only include the quantities desired and a schedule; later, for a more accurate estimate, the manufacturing plan should be more detailed. The plan should state production quantities and schedules with a fabrication and assembly sequence diagram and with a list of the major tooling, test equipment, and other facilities. Manufacturing personnel requirements, along with any unusual training or recruiting ideas, should be stated. The estimator should ask about these subjects and make the answers part of the documentation of the estimate. If possible, the manufacturing department, rather than the LCC analyst, should prepare the manufacturing plan. The plan does not have to be for a unique situation; a number of production quantities could be specified, or different schedules could be considered. Cost estimates would then be prepared for each alternative.

Elements of Cost

The elements of cost categorize various sources of costs. A brief review of such standard elements follows.[2]

Nonrecurring and Recurring Costs

In manufacturing, a number of costs are incurred only once, at the beginning of the production run. These include tooling, test equipment, manufacturing planning, new facilities, training, and recruitment. Such *nonrecurring costs* are roughly independent of the quantity to be produced. They are to be distinguished from repetitive or *recurring costs* that are incurred for each item or each month of production. Recurring costs include manufacturing labor, material, inspection, and tool and machine maintenance. Estimate non-recurring and recurring costs separately, the nonrecurring costs as a total, and the recurring costs on a per unit or a per month basis. The recurring costs may then be multiplied by the desired production quantities to obtain the total cost estimate.

Nonrecurring and recurring costs may overlap; the distinction is often fuzzy. For example, the quantity and quality of tooling (and therefore its cost) change with any large changes in production quantity and rates. This nonrecurring tooling cost may then vary with respect to production quantities. Similarly, the recurring costs may change with production quantities, simulating a fixed initial cost. For relatively small changes in production quantities (less than a factor of two), the nonrecurring and recurring cost factors can be considered constant.

Direct and Indirect Costs

Recurring and nonrecurring costs are charged directly to a particular product or contract. But some costs are difficult to attach to a specific product. For example, because it is difficult to assess the cost of electrical power and other utilities for each product, these are considered *indirect costs.* Customarily, building maintenance, supervision, purchasing agents, clerical help, and personnel and accounting departments are not charged to specific products. Their costs are accumulated and apportioned to each product as *departmental overhead,* or more generally, *overhead.* Overhead is usually apportioned as a percentage of a product's direct costs and may vary from 75 percent to 150 percent. The overhead burden is usually applied to the direct departments, such as manufacturing and engineering, during all contract phases, including research and development as well as production.

Allocated direct charges. Some production costs cannot

conveniently be charged directly to a product, nor are they indirect, overhead costs. The heat-treating furnaces and the paint and finishing operation handle many products each day. Their work on an individual product is part of its specific, constructive manufacturing operations, but a separate accounting for each as it passes through the operation would be costly. Therefore such costs are often handled as "allocated direct charges": they are distributed as a proportion of some other direct charges, such as direct labor.

Overtime Allowance

Most programs sooner or later encounter problems that require the use of overtime or other premium labor. After estimating the cost of all direct labor, use a multiplying factor (between 5 and 10 percent) to allow for the probable use of overtime; this factor may be different for the different phases or different departments. If the schedule is tight, or manpower short, or the customer capricious and demanding, the overtime requirement will probably be higher, and the multiplying factor must be adjusted accordingly.

General and Admininistrative Costs

The cost of general management, the corporate counsel, public relations, and similar functions not identified with a particular department are often grouped into another "burden" account that is charged to each product. This burden is called general and administrative overhead costs and is applied as a proportion of the total direct and indirect charges from all direct charging departments; the factor may vary from 5 to 50 percent, depending on the accounting system used.

Profit

The motive for all this effort is the pursuit of profit, and it should not be forgotten. After all costs for any contract have been estimated, the profit (or fee) should be added. This final total is the price.

The amount of fee allowable on government contracts varies with the contractor's investment, the risks incurred, and other factors. Competition is always an influence. In the absence of other information, 12 percent should be estimated.

Estimating Methods

The three basic methods of estimating research and development costs also apply to production costs. These methods are related, complement each other, and even seem to merge into a progression. Analogy, initially at a high level, yields a rough order-of-magnitude cost. With refinements of the analogy, the product is subdivided and various functional relationships develop between product characteristics and cost. If these functional relationships are expressed mathematically, they are aggrandized as cost-estimating relations. Several specialists, each working on a part of the estimate, produce what is called grass roots, bottom up, or industrial engineering estimates. But each one estimates by analogy, relying on past experience, either intuitively or explicitly, at a lower, more detailed level. They estimate a particular task by comparing it to previous tasks on other programs. All estimating, therefore, is done on the basis of past experience.

What if past experience is not available for a job? The classic and still usable approach is to break down the job into recognizable tasks. The level of analysis may be as basic as the hand motions of an individual worker, but a higher level of analysis is preferable, such as a machine tool operation or the manufacture of a subassembly. The overall estimate then consists of the sum of the estimates of these familiar tasks.

Analogy

Each of the elements of cost enumerated above can be

estimated by analogy to previous production. Usually, analogy is used for the price (or cost) as a whole. A similar product is found, differences between the new product and the old product are analyzed, and the cost is adjusted accordingly. The *power law* attempts to adjust the differences by a mathematical equation:

$$\text{Cost} = C_o \left(\frac{P_n}{P_o} \right)^s$$

where Cost = Cost of the new product

P$_n$ = Controlling parameter of the new product

P$_o$ = Controlling parameter of the old product

C$_o$ = Cost of the old product

s = The power factor

If a new pump of ten horsepower were to be estimated and if it were known that a five-horsepower pump cost $200, this relationship could be used. The power factor varies between 0 and 1, and 0.5 is a reasonable first approximation. In this case, the cost of the new pump would be $283. Other factors would have to be used for changes in production quantity or for changes in other performance measures.[3]

Estimates by analogy should use more than one analogous item whenever possible. If a similar product cannot be found, perhaps products comparable to parts of the new product can be found. A table such as Table 3-1 might be set up comparing the costs of similar products to various parts of the new product, with notes as to differences. Clifton Trigg has detailed such a procedure for estimation by analogy.[4]

Cost-Estimating Relations

Manufacturing costs are occasionally estimated by CERs.

Table 3-1
ESTIMATING PRODUCTION COSTS
BY ANALOGY
(All costs include overhead but not fee)

STRUCTURE:

Analogous Equipment. Model X structure cost was $110 per pound at the 100th aircraft.

New Aircraft. Uses more welding; fabrication cost equal, but X-ray inspection adds 10 percent.

Titanium at twice the cost is used in engine areas which are 5 percent of the total; add 10 percent.

Estimate new structure at $110 X 1.1 X 1.1 $132 per pound at the 100th aircraft.

AVIONICS:

Analogous Equipment. Model Y installed avionics cost was $800,000. Model Z installed cost was $1,500,000.

New Aircraft. Improved high-temperature capability required over Model Y; adds 15 percent (vendor telephonic estimate).

Deletes one communication band from Model Y; decreases 3 percent (engineering estimate).

Deletes about half of Model Z capability (engineering estimate).

Estimate new avionics based on Model Y at $896,000.

Estimate new avionics based on Model Z at $750,000.

Model Y analogy closer and more dependable; use $850,000.

The most basic CER relates total cost to direct labor cost. This suggests that material costs and overhead costs are proportional to the amount of direct labor involved. For initial calculations in the missile and electronics industry, total costs are about three times the direct labor cost. For aircraft manufacturing (which is more labor-intensive), a multiplier of two is often used. In a highly automated manufacturing facility, the multiplier might be four or more.

The direct labor required is estimated as proportional to the weight of the product, or the total amount of machining to be done, or the total number of electronic components to be mounted. Manufacturing CERs are peculiar to a par-

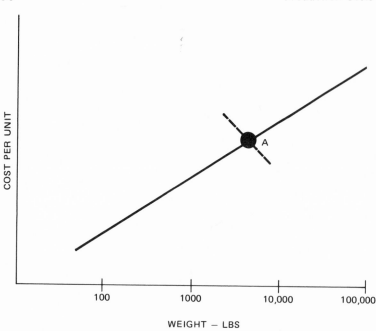

Figure 3-1. Macroscopic vs. Microscopic View of CER

ticular industry; the CER is associated with a particular product and the way it is manufactured. In the aircraft industry, for many years the total aircraft weight was used, with the multiplying constant different for fighter aircraft, bombers, commercial transports, and so on. This same procedure has been used for missiles and other military equipment. For missiles, the basic-weight CER has been refined by the Naval Weapons Center, China Lake, to include such factors as range, guidance frequency, antenna diameter, maximum speed, total booster impulse, payload fraction, and environmental requirements.

The most fully developed set of such CERs is contained in the RCA PRICE computer model, which has been successfully used for electronic products and a wide variety of other manufactured items. Starting with the weight, the model modifies the cost according to the manufacturing com-

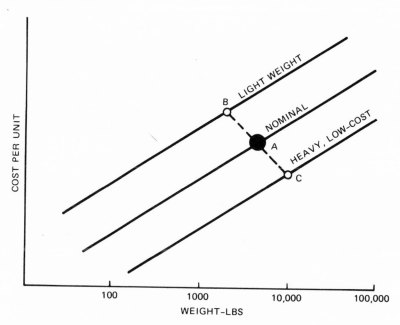

Figure 3-2. Family of CERs

plexity, the production quantity, the environmental specifications, the year of production, the number of changes expected, the proportion of electronic to mechanical weight,
and programmatic factors. An experienced and skilled user
can achieve accuracies of better than 10 percent of the production cost.

For the chemical industry, F. C. Jelen has published a
number of helpful relationships.[5] Other CERs have been
developed, but many originating organizations try not to
disclose them for competitive reasons.

A paradox. The simple CER relating weight and cost is
illustrated in Figure 3-1. The line sloping up from southwest
to northeast is conventional and well accepted at first glance.
If, however, a designer has to lighten a design, which is at
point *A*, the cost will invariably increase. The slope rises from
southeast to northwest, just the opposite of the accepted,

macro line. If the designer is asked to decrease the cost from point *A,* some weight penalty is sure to be involved. Again, the line slopes from northwest to southeast, opposite to the accepted line. Is this micro behavior a contradiction or refutation of the CER? Not at all. Figure 3-2 shows a set of relationships between a product and its weight with two additional lines added to the original, single, nominal relationship of Figure 3-1. These show a lightweight design and a less expensive design with some weight penalty. An ultralightweight design line could be added, as well as other variations, to give a whole family of lines. The retrograde micro line in Figure 3-1 now moves from *A* on the nominal line to *B* on the lightweight line or to *C* on the low-cost line.

The above procedures are relatively easy to develop in theory, but developing the specific quantitative relations, such as the PRICE model, takes a great deal of work and many years before acceptance by others is achieved.

Industrial Engineering Production Estimating

As in R&D cost estimating, the industrial engineering method calls for an itemized estimate of the production costs. In contrast to the R&D estimating process, the personnel who will do the tasks (manufacturing) are not usually asked to prepare the estimate, though foremen and other supervisors may be approached for some judgments.

The industrial engineering method is the most widely used procedure for production estimating. The method starts with a listing of the cost of each component (the bill of materials), as the lowest level of detail available, and then adds the cost of the assembly and test operation to obtain the total cost. This total includes the direct fabrication labor, which is usually estimated by standard hours and adjusted by learning curves, quality assurance labor, and materials and other manufacturing support.

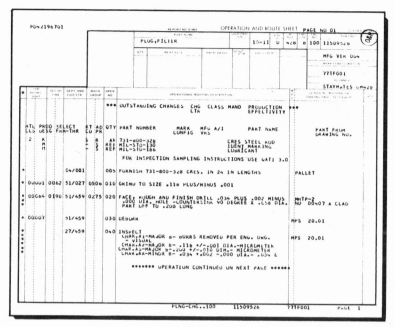

Figure 3-3.   Individual Tasks in the
Manufacturing Planning

Standard hours. Many organizations have prepared lists of standard tasks and the time required to do them. The time requirements have been developed by time study methods and methods time measurement (MTM) dating back to the nineteenth century. The tasks range from simple ones such as "inserting a screw" to more complex ones such as "turning a rough casting in lathe," to still larger ones, such as "vibration test assembly." LCC estimators should adopt the standard tasks used for shop instructions in the manufacturing planning (Figure 3-3) and should determine from the standard hours book how much time is required for each step of the planning. The total of all these steps is the direct labor for the item. Note that this estimate is for some arbitrary point in the production program, usually the 100th or 1,000th unit.

The standard hours include a small allowance for lost time (personal time, unavoidable delays, interruptions). Even so, the standard hours are seldom realized in factory operations. The ratio of the calculated standard hours to the actual hours required to do the job is called the *realization rate.* The realization rate varies from company to company, shop to shop, and time to time, but it rarely exceeds 85 percent and on occasion may drop to as little as 15 percent. Subjective judgments of the realization rate can, and often do, change estimates dramatically. Thus the original direct labor cost must be divided by the expected realization rate (or multiplied by the inverse, the ratio of actual to standard). The result is the direct, hands-on labor cost. To this must be added the cost of other direct labor (quality assurance, production conrol, material handling, manufacturing engineering) to obtain the total direct labor cost.

The use of standard hours is accepted and widespread but poses some difficulties. For example:

1. The upkeep of the standard time book is expensive.
2. The data are often obsolete, and trends are difficult to detect.
3. A great deal of time is required to provide the required level of detail for estimating, which may be impossible early in the program.
4. An estimate based at a higher level of assembly may obscure cost differences between alternative manufacturing methods.

The method of costing standard hours is quite straightforward. To obtain the direct labor cost, multiply the estimated actual hours by the wage rate. The current hourly wage rate may be adjusted for expected inflation, possible new union contracts, or other changes. Use either a gross average wage rate or individual wage rates for various tasks and skill levels organizations.

Learning curves. The amount of effort required to manufacture an item decreases with each successive item produced: workers become more skillful; better tools, improved manufacturing methods, better materials and designs become available and so on. Production people have been aware of this "learning curve" for a long time. During World War II, the aircraft manufacturing industry discovered that the average effort (man-hours) needed to produce an initial group of aircraft could be reduced by a fixed proportion in the next group of that same number of aircraft. For example, if the first five aircraft had been produced at an average of 1,000 man-hours each, that average would fall to, say, 900 man-hours after the production of another five aircraft. T. P. Wright termed this the 90 percent cumulative average learning curve.[6] It meant, of course, that the second five aircraft had to be produced at an average of 800 man-hours each (the tenth aircraft would require even fewer). With each successive doubling of production, the required man-hours continued to decrease by enough to decrease the cumulative average by 90 percent. The 90 percent value was widely used in the aircraft manufacturing industry and became almost obligatory. Note than an 80 percent learning curve requires still more improvement as each item is produced. The lower the number, the more learning effect is assumed.

The learning curve may be expressed as an equation:

$$E = K N^S$$

E =   Average effort for production of N units, usually in man-hours

K =   The effort to produce the first unit

N =   The number of units produced

s =   The learning curve constant

Because of the exponential relationship, the data are often plotted on log-log graph paper where the values show as a

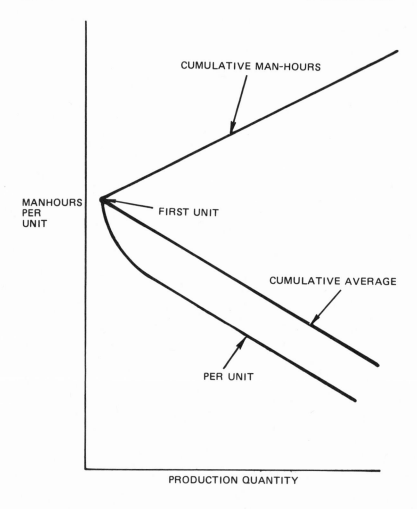

Figure 3 – 4.   Manufacturing Learning Curve, Wright

straight line, as in Figure 3-4.

A second type of learning curve is also used, based on the cost per unit. This method, introduced by James R. Craw-ford,[7] states that the *unit cost* will follow a straight line on log-log graph paper (Figure 3-5). The slope of this line and the stated learning curve value (in percent) differ from the cumulative average learning curve. In using values of learning

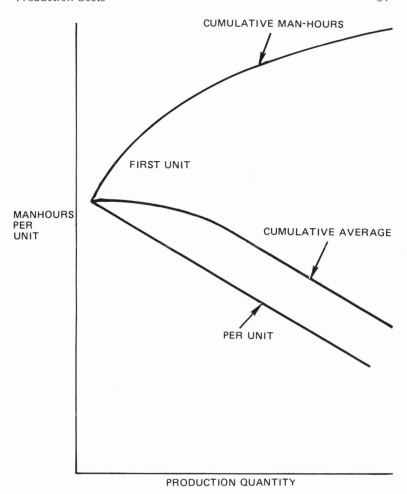

Figure 3-5. Manufacturing Learning Curve, Crawford

curve constants, be sure not to confuse cumulative average values with unit values.

The learning rate varies in different manufacturing operations. Highly automated operations tend to show less learning than those with much manual labor. Actual experience will vary, seemingly dependent on management's commitment to improving costs. A concerted effort to improve methods, tooling, training, and individual motivation can transform the operation from a marginal 95 percent learning curve to a creditable 75 percent curve. An interesting side effect of awareness of this learning curve is that because workers expect a decrease in production effort they try to achieve it.

The base value used to start the learning curve is obtained by the standard hours method discussed earlier. This standard hours method, as mentioned, will usually be for the 100th or 1,000th unit, which is easily converted to the required constant for the learning curve equation.

Note that much of the learning may be lost if there is a break in production. The amount of loss will depend on the length of the break and the efforts made to retain know-how. Similarly, design changes may impede progress toward lower rates. A number of texts provide detailed methods and procedures for using the learning curve technique.[8] These provide tables and calculation methods using graphical techniques. Calculators, now widely available, provide the most exact method of using the equation, however.[9]

Plant capacity. The amount of the plant in use has a significant effect on costs. Fixed costs, by definition, continue even if only part of the plant is busy. Therefore, in estimating costs, it may be necessary to forecast the workload for the entire plant. If the plant is running at less than capacity, it is necessary to impose a new and higher overhead burden on the calculated direct charges.

Quality assurance. The cost of inspection and other quality assurance activities is added to the manufacturing costs. Inspection is a recurring cost and is handled like other direct labor costs. Many estimators calculate inspection as a percentage of manufacturing direct labor; 8 percent is usual for military hardware. Quality planning and some other quality engineering activities are nonrecurring, direct costs. Statistical analysis is a recurring, direct cost. For a crude, overall estimate, traditional quality costs have been 10 percent of total manufacturing costs. As quality assurance has been able to demonstrate its cost prevention worth, some organizations have allocated larger amounts to quality activities.

Manufacturing support. In most manufacturing operations, a number of support operations other than quality assurance are direct costs. These include:

1. manufacturing engineering for the maintenance of tool design, manufacturing methods, and planning
2. engineering liaison for design interpretations and changes
3. the material review board for the disposition of discrepant material
4. failure diagnosis of test failures by engineers and technicians to determine the cause
5. testing of incoming parts prior to installation
6. tooling and test equipment maintenance and calibration
7. production and material control
8. material handling within the plant

These are estimated either as a proportion of the manufacturing direct labor hours or on the basis of the particular task. For order-of-magnitude estimates, 10 to 30 percent of the manufacturing direct labor cost should cover these areas. For an individual program, however, some of the functions may be omitted or specially augmented. If the quality assurance requirements are particularly difficult, the material review task may be larger than usual. If the production rates are low, the manufacturing engineering task may be a larger proportion of manufacturing hours than usual. The cost estimate should be adjusted to recognize such differences.

In using one of the three methods of cost estimation, be sure to state its underlying justification and basis, as outlined in Table 3-2. The credibility of the estimate is enhanced by such backup information. In order to answer subsequent

Table 3-2
JUSTIFICATION AND BASIS FOR ESTIMATES

I Analogy
  A. Identify the analogous item and justify the specific
      analogy.
  B. Provide historical costs for a specific production quantity;
      explain the use of learning curves to adjust quantities.
  C. Explain adjustment factors used such as the power law.
      Identify all changes to the analogous item and their
      impact on costs.

II Cost-Estimating Relations
  A. Provide the CER.
  B. Discuss the form of the equation used and its basis, e.g.,
      empirical, physical laws, or experience.
  C. Identify the historical data on which the CER is based.
  D. Provide statistical methods used, confidence levels found,
      and other measures of reliability.

III Industrial Engineering
  A. Provide vendor quotations with names, ranges of bids,
      and justify vendors selected.
  B. Provide list of tasks, standard hours, wage rates, realization
      rates and learning curves.
  C. Specify additional tasks such as quality assurance, manu-
      facturing engineering, testing, and program management
      and methods of estimating these.
  D. List nonrecurring costs such as tooling and tool design,
      and methods of estimating these.

questions, the estimator should have in his personal files
backup data at an even greater level of detail.

Purchased Material Estimating

In many industries, the purchased material component is
the largest part of the sales price. This may vary from 50 percent in labor-intensive industries such as aircraft and electronics to 80 percent in distributing firms where there is
relatively little value added. The proportion is relatively

stable for a particular industry and so can be used as a CER. If the material requirements are known, then the total sales price can be calculated by dividing the material cost by the material percentage. If the direct labor is known, the material costs are again a fixed percentage, and the total sales price can be estimated.

For a detailed industrial engineering estimate, material costs can be estimated from catalogs or price sheets when standard items or raw stock are bought. One or more suppliers may be asked for a quotation. Most suppliers are happy to furnish such quotations and consider these as firm commitments for a short period of time. They may be reluctant to quote prices, however, if they suspect that the potential buyer will decide to fabricate the item in his own facility. Suppliers are reluctant to compete against the buyer's organization. In such circumstances, do not expect the usual cooperation from suppliers' estimators; they are unusually sensitive to this situation because their survival depends on it.

Material Burden

Accounting departments differ as to whether the cost of purchased material should be burdened with departmental overhead costs. The argument in favor states that the purchasing department, material control, and others involved with material are part of departmental overhead and that the expense of these departments should be added to the cost of material. The opposition replies that material requires relatively little in the way of overhead services. A more equitable way of distributing the departmental overhead is in proportion to the direct labor charges. The Cost Accounting Standards Board has recently decided the issue for U.S. government suppliers with the issuance of CAS 410, which states that material will have overhead applied. The jury is still out on this question, and various accounting departments disagree; either method, consistently applied, works.

Customer Costs

During the production phase, the customer incurs a number of costs. The program management office is larger than during the R&D phase, various technical advisory groups will be supported, testing programs are expanded, training becomes larger, transportation to more distant locations is needed, and development models may need to be refurbished or brought up to the production configuration. With these customer costs added to the production costs, the total for the investment phase can be obtained.

Training Costs

The instructors trained during R&D may start to train the crews for operational test evaluations. These crews will need manuals, training facilities, training aids, and so on. The major cost is the cost of the instructors' and the students' time. Methods of estimating such costs will be discussed in Chapter 4.

Test Costs

Customer test costs will expand during the production phase, including both acceptance tests of production and field qualification tests. A test plan is needed to outline these requirements before any costing can be done. As noted in Chapter 2, test costs include the test facility (test ranges, ships, aircraft, wind tunnels, proving grounds), test personnel, the items under test, targets, and supporting personnel (data reduction and analysis, security, communications). For a test program using ships or aircraft, the qualification test program can cost several hundreds of thousands of dollars per month. Targets for weapons testing can be particularly expensive. Costs for targets can be obtained from vendors, from previous procurements, or can be estimated using the methods outlined in this chapter.

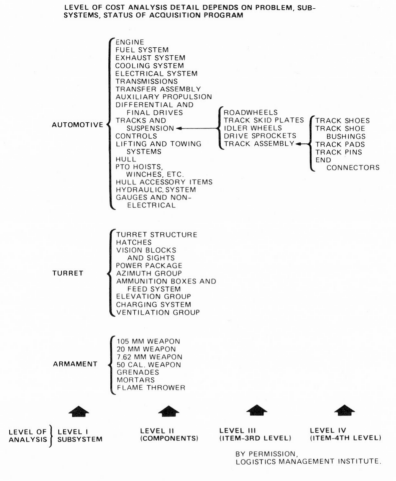

LEVEL OF COST ANALYSIS DETAIL DEPENDS ON PROBLEM, SUB-
SYSTEMS, STATUS OF ACQUISITION PROGRAM

AUTOMOTIVE
- ENGINE
- FUEL SYSTEM
- EXHAUST SYSTEM
- COOLING SYSTEM
- ELECTRICAL SYSTEM
- TRANSMISSIONS
- TRANSFER ASSEMBLY
- AUXILIARY PROPULSION
- DIFFERENTIAL AND FINAL DRIVES
- TRACKS AND SUSPENSION
  - ROADWHEELS
  - TRACK SKID PLATES
  - IDLER WHEELS
  - DRIVE SPROCKETS
  - TRACK ASSEMBLY
    - TRACK SHOES
    - TRACK SHOE BUSHINGS
    - TRACK PADS
    - TRACK PINS
    - END CONNECTORS
- CONTROLS
- LIFTING AND TOWING SYSTEMS
- HULL
- PTO HOISTS, WINCHES, ETC.
- HULL ACCESSORY ITEMS
- HYDRAULIC SYSTEM
- GAUGES AND NON-ELECTRICAL

TURRET
- TURRET STRUCTURE
- HATCHES
- VISION BLOCKS AND SIGHTS
- POWER PACKAGE
- AZIMUTH GROUP
- AMMUNITION BOXES AND FEED SYSTEM
- ELEVATION GROUP
- CHARGING SYSTEM
- VENTILATION GROUP

ARMAMENT
- 105 MM WEAPON
- 20 MM WEAPON
- 7.62 MM WEAPON
- 50 CAL. WEAPON
- GRENADES
- MORTARS
- FLAME THROWER

| LEVEL OF ANALYSIS | LEVEL I SUBSYSTEM | LEVEL II (COMPONENTS) | LEVEL III (ITEM-3RD LEVEL) | LEVEL IV (ITEM-4TH LEVEL) |

BY PERMISSION,
LOGISTICS MANAGEMENT INSTITUTE.

Figure 3-6. WBS is Progressively Defined to Lower Levels

Transportation

Production costs are usually estimated and quoted by contractors as FOB the factory. Transportation to the customer acceptance point, and then to the point of use, should be added to the contractor's costs. A rough order-of-magnitude estimate for domestic shipment is $1 per pound, and for overseas shipment, $2 per pound. Clearly, a more accurate estimate is possible if the shipment destination and method of shipment (air, ship, truck, or rail) are known and if packaging requirements are defined. Transportation costs are usually not large enough to warrant any major, early estimating effort. This topic is discussed in further detail in Chapter 5.

Facilities

During the production phase, the customer may need a number of facilities. See Chapter 5 for a discussion of how to estimate these.

Work Breakdown Structure

The work breakdown structure (WBS) discussed in Chapter 2 should be carefully followed for the production estimate. It should be defined down to lower and lower levels as the system becomes better known so that more precise estimates can be made (see Figure 3-6). This will be continued in the operation and support phase, so that the WBS becomes more and more complete, and the LCC estimate correspondingly more dependable.

Summary

A manufacturing plan is needed to estimate manufacturing costs. A gross estimate of production cost can be made by analogy. CERs are not generally available for production costs, except for the RCA PRICE model. The industrial engineering method can provide accurate labor estimates using standard hours, a realization rate, and learning curves. Material costs are estimated as a proportion of labor costs or from a bill of materials. These direct costs are burdened with overhead and general administrative expenses. After adding overtime allowance and profit, the resultant total production price is added to the other customer costs to obtain the total investment required.

Notes

1. Phillip Ostwald, *Cost Estimating for Engineering and Management* (Englewood Cliffs, N.J.: Prentice-Hall, 1974); Carl J. Gobis, *Tool, Die and Industrial Estimating: Estimators Handbook* (Detroit: Estimators Handbook, 1968); Paul F. Gallagher, *Project Estimating by Engineering Methods* (New York: Hayden Book, 1965), particularly good for electronics, with learning curves; Ivan R. Vernon, *Realistic Cost Estimating for Manufacturing* (Dearborn, Mich.: American Society of Tool and Manufacturing Engineers, 1968); Stephen A. Tucker, *Cost-Estimating and Pricing with Machine Hour Rates* (Engelwood Cliffs, N.J.: Prentice-Hall, 1962).

2. Gordon Shillinglaw, *Cost Accounting: Analysis and Control* (Homewood, Ill.: Richard D. Irwin, 1972).

3. Ostwald, *Cost Estimating*, gives a good discussion of the power law.

4. Clifton T. Trigg, *Guidelines for Cost Estimation by Analogy*, ECOM-4125 (Ft. Monmouth, N.J.: U.S. Army Electronics Command, 1973).

5. F. C. Jelen, *Cost and Optimization Engineering* (New York: McGraw-Hill, for the American Association of Cost Engineers, 1970).

6. Gallagher, *Project Estimating*, pp. 25-30.

7. Ibid., pp. 28-32.

8. Ibid., pp. 32-50; and Ravinder Nanda and George L. Adler, eds., *Learning Curves Theory and Application* (Norcross, Ga.: American Institute of Industrial Engineers, 1978).

9. Frederick M. Garver, "Putting Learning Curves in Your Pocket," *Industrial Engineering*, June 1977.

4
Operating and Support Costs

Operating and support (O&S) costs are usually the largest part of LCC. Operating costs are incurred during the use of an item (personnel, fuel, and operating support), and support costs are those for maintenance, provisioning, support equipment, training, technical manuals, and other nonoperating support functions (site preparation and installation and security requirements). Analysis of these costs requires an understanding of the various methods of employment, maintenance, and logistics. LCC analysis can show how to select the best of these methods so as to minimize costs. In order to show how to allocate and control these costs, this chapter will expand the work breakdown structure to a matrix format.

O&S costs are incurred during the O&S phase. Some agencies divide this into two phases: (1) *deployment,* including the initial, nonrecurring costs of training, provisioning, and so on; and (2) *operations and recurring support* for the continuing costs during the use of the item. Because the distinction between these costs is not clear, the more inclusive term *O&S* will be used here.

Because O&S costs are the largest part of LCC, they require critical examination. The uncertainty of such estimates is occasionally advanced as a reason for not estimating them at all. But this is precisely why they should be estimated, for the estimating process reduces the uncertainty of the numbers. The estimating steps require analysts to plan deployment, maintenance procedures, provisioning, training and recruitment, and support equipment. The computation in dollars of the necessary logistic resources for a system provides a common measure to use in evaluating such resource requirements. This is an iterative process, repeated and refined as the program continues.

O&S costs depend on how much an item is used. The more it is used, the higher the costs. For military items, use and costs are highest in wartime, but wartime operations are very difficult to predict (and obtain a consensus on) and are not really needed to develop cost planning. Weapon systems are employed and supported during peacetime in ways that simulate combat operations; reserves of ammunition and other provisions are maintained. These costs are made a part of LCC. Therefore, most LCC estimates are based on peacetime operations and do not attempt to predict the likelihood of combat or its duration.

Operating Costs

The first step is to draw up an operations plan with a statement of the operating sequence of the weapon system, a description of the operating environment and the force structure, and a schedule for deployment and use. Because personnel costs are usually the major cost driver, the operations plan must provide enough information to determine the quantity and skill levels of personnel needed. The plan also should include a factory-to-target sequence, like that in Figure 4-1, to sketch the basis of the logistics plan. Operating costs are directly required during the use of an item; support costs include maintenance, training, and other nonoperating functions.

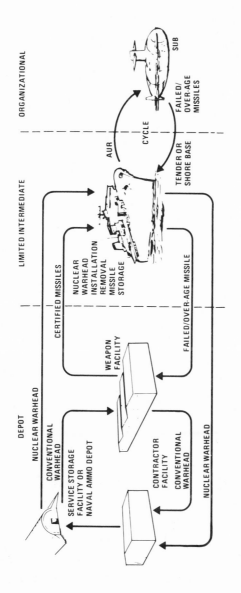

Figure 4-1. Factory to Target Sequence

Table 4-1
MILITARY PERSONNEL COSTS, 1978

Grade	Pay and Allowances	Billet
E-2	6,625	15,381
E-3	6,976	15,907
E-4	7,927	17,782
E-5	9,277	23,771
E-6	11,173	31,224
E-7	13,445	36,090
E-8	15,659	40,475
O-1	11,111	27,811
O-2	14,722	35,414
O-3	18,908	40,013

Operating Personnel

To obtain the cost of operating personnel, multiply the number of assigned people in each grade by the cost per grade per unit of time, and by the time periods covered. The simplest but incomplete way to express the cost of military personnel is in terms of the "pay and allowances" of each person involved. Sample values of pay and allowances for 1978 are given in the middle column in Table 4-1. Because these values omit all of the other costs required to have a person available at an operational billet, the right-hand column on billet costs includes the cost of training the person, his nonproductive time (as patient or transient), the cost of recruitment, and the cost of retirement. In other words, the cost of personnel used in LCC estimates should be calculated using billet costs, as in Table 4-1. If the pay and allowances values are used, billet costs should be obtained by using a multiplying factor or by adding other personnel cost categories, such as training and medical services. The three services provide this personnel cost information in their cost planning documents.[1]

Note that these military personnel costs do not include higher command costs such as headquarters, staff office, and so on. These are not usually included in LCC estimates of a particular item.

If the operators are civilians (a rare situation), their costs are the estimated contract costs, e.g., $60,000 per man-year. For civil service personnel, their salary plus an overhead allowance (100 percent?) can be used.

Number of operators. Many systems, such as tanks, aircraft, ships, and missiles, fully occupy the time of the staff assigned to them. In these cases, the number of operating personnel is the number of assigned people. Shipboard systems, aircraft systems, or many ground stations, however, may employ personnel on a part-time or irregular basis. Men who are available to operate a particular system but are not actively working on it should not be fully charged to the system. They are available to work on another system, or they may be on unpaid standby status. In either case, the analyst should calculate what proportion of the operator's time should be charged against the system under consideration. For example, a navy gun system may have an assigned crew of four. If certain recommended procedural changes are made, however, the workload may be reduced so that a crew of 3.3 men would be sufficient. Navy practice is to continue to assign four men to the gun crew; but, for LCC purposes, the available surplus time of the 0.7 man (4 minus 3.3) should not be charged against the gun, for it can be used for other duties aboard ship.

Finally, in many systems the operator also does some minor maintenance. The usual practice is to charge such

operators against operating costs alone without attempting to
divide their time between operating and maintenance costs.
The total O&S costs are, of course, unaffected.

Petroleum, Oil, and Lubricants

The operations plan should specify at what speeds, over
what distances, and for how long the system will operate.
The force structure provides the number of operating units.
Using the conventional factors of fuel consumed per mile or
per hour, fuel needs can be calculated by multiplication.
Alternatively, data may be available on the average fuel consumption per day for a fleet of trucks, planes, ships, or other
equipment. This latter method may be a better approximation because it averages usage over a number of vehicles. The
category of petroleum, oils, and lubricants (POL) includes
products other than fuel. These costs are often taken as a
ratio of the fuel used. Detailed information on the particular
vehicle used may make it possible to refine this CER.

POL data are readily available from the planning factors
manuals.[2] The cost of POL in containers and in bulk is also
available.[3] Usually, more detailed information is required.
The services often do not have servicewide data available in a
format useful to the LCC analyst; servicewide data are highly
aggregated. For example, there may be figures on total automotive use of fuel in the army, or for a division, but no information on the fuel consumption of a particular vehicle. Individual operating organizations, however, often do have data
on the fuel consumption of each model of their tanks, ships,
or other vehicles. The motor pool officer may not know precisely how many miles were traveled but can make a good
approximation, and specific fuel consumption can be calculated from that. He will usually know the total amount of
lubricants used and can guess the respective allocations to
trucks, tanks, or other units. Obtaining these data takes
individual visits or correspondence, and careful judgment is

required to decide if the results can be generalized. Failing all else, the manufacturer's data can be helpful, but they must be studied to make sure that they apply to the particular situation.

Other Consumables

Weapon systems may use such diverse consumables as liquid nitrogen, ammunition, amd bombs. These are estimated in the same way as POL requirements. The initial problem is to determine the extent of a system's use. During peacetime, the only operations are for training (or perhaps display). Mobilization and similar maneuvers are considered wartime situations and are not used in LCC estimates, as noted earlier. The operations plan should estimate the number of hours the system operates per year; knowledge of the characteristics of the system makes it possible to calculate the use of consumables such as liquid nitrogen. Other consumables, such as ammunition and bombs, may be used only for test and evaluation and training; the test and training plans provide a basis for these estimates. Supplies for personnel, such as food, uniforms, tools, medicine, and so on, are given in the planning factors handbooks.[4]

War reserve. The army, for one, includes the cost of a war reserve in calculations of LCC. This provides a way of costing some combat operations without trying to predict the future. The war reserve is defined as the quantity of ammunition and other consumables needed for a fixed period of time during a prescribed combat scenario. For example, the war reserve might include the amount of ammunition a battalion of air defense guns would need for four air defense engagements per day over a ninety-day period. The cost of such a stockpile, including procurement, storage, and handling, would be included in the LCC. The size of the war reserve depends on the number of targets to be destroyed, so that the most effective air defense gun is the one that destroys the most targets with the least ammunition, thereby reducing costs. Thus, designers try to improve the gun by decreasing the amount of ammunition it uses, but such improvements in design, manufacture, and O&S expenses obviously must not cost more than the savings in consumables such as ammunition.

A design cost trade-off will show whether certain design alternatives generate net savings. For example, assume that it would be possible to increase the single-shot kill probability of an air defense gun from 0.1 to 0.2 at a cost of $5 million in nonrecurring costs, plus $50,000 per weapon in recurring costs. Assume also that ammunition costs $20 per round, that each weapon sees four targets per day for ninety days and that the desired engagement kill probability for a target is 0.9. For a 0.9 engagement kill probability, with a single-shot kill probability of 0.1, twenty rounds are needed. For the same 0.9 engagement kill probability, with a single-shot kill probability of 0.2, only eleven rounds are needed:

Ammo. Cost $(P_k = .1)$ (4) x (90) x (22) x (20)	$158,400 per weapon
Ammo. Cost $(P_k = .2)$ (4) x (90) x (11) x (20)	$ 79,200 per weapon
Ammo. Cost difference	$ 79,200

Weapons fielded	100	200
Weapon Cost Increase	$10,000,000	$15,000,000
Ammo. Cost saving	$ 7,920,000	$15,840,000
Net saving (deficit)	($ 2,080,000)	$ 840,000

For a total procurement of 100 guns, the improved kill probability would cost $2,080,000; for a total procurement of 200 guns, the improved kill probability would save $840,000. The break-even point is about 172 guns. If it is planned to produce and field at least 172 weapons, it would be worthwhile to improve the single-shot kill probability. Additional cost trade-offs will be discussed in detail in Chapter 9.

Operating Support

The operation of a weapon system may require external support systems, some of which can be very expensive. Naval aircraft require aircraft carriers; army antiaircraft systems must have command and control networks; space systems use tracking information of satellites; and air defense systems call for radar warning networks. If the support system already exists and if the alternative possibilities use it equally, it need not be costed in the LCC estimates. A cost-sharing arrangement is often used to allocate the proportionate share of the support system to the weapon under consideration. LCC ground rules should state explicitly how such support system costs are handled. For example, a new naval aircraft might not bear any share of the cost of the naval carriers; a new antiaircraft system might bear all of the costs of modifying the command and control network for the new demands on it; a space system might assume 40 percent of the cost of the computer that provides satellite tracking information.

The cost-estimating process for support systems is the same as for weapon systems. In many cases, funds have already been spent for R&D and procurement of the support system. These are sunk costs and should be mentioned, but they are not summed into the LCC.

Support Costs

Support costs are the largest part of the O&S spending, and maintenance requirements generate most support costs. Only standby or dormant systems, such as some missile systems, may be an exception to the rule. Maintenance labor, provisioning, training, technical manuals, and support equipment are used primarily for maintaining equipment. Planning for these resources should be integrated with other logistics requirements, for both operations and support.

Integrated Logistic Support Plan

The LCC estimator needs a description of the logistic support for the weapon system (or other item); as before, one of the many benefits of an LCC analysis is that it stimulates integrated logistic support (ILS) planning. The integrated logistic support plan should include all the support considerations needed during the life cycle of a system; principal elements are (1) the maintenance plan, (2) the support and test equipment plan, (3) supply support, (4) transportation and handling, (5) technical data, (6) facilities, (7) personnel and training, (8) logistic support funds funding, and (9) logistics support management information. In some programs, of course, some elements listed may not be large enough to warrant the discussion. The evaluation of such a plan in money terms always forces careful consideration and prevents generalities. (A description of the content of an ILS plan may be found in DOD Directive 4100.35.)[5]

The integrated logistic support plan is based on a logistic scenario, which provides the broad outlines for the system's support. Are failed components repaired? Who does the repair? Where will the supplies come from? When? During production or later? Where will they be stored? How will supplies be transported, both routinely and in emergencies? What kinds of maintenance or other personnel will be needed? Where will they be trained? What training facilities are available, and what new ones will be needed? The answers to these questions are never final, but all should be dealt with in a baseline support scenario. Changes in this initial plan can be considered later and accepted or rejected after their costs have been evaluated. Note that it is necessary to start from a baseline plan, because the comparison of a number of different complete support concepts is time-consuming and it is difficult to discern which characteristic change can be separately considered.

The ILS plan starts with a maintenance plan as a means of

discovering what maintenance resources (manpower, spares and repair parts, tools and test equipment, training and technical manuals) are needed. After itemizing these resources, the logistic analyst should examine the weapon-system design to determine whether some resource requirements can be eliminated or reduced by design change. This is a continuation of the cost optimization and cost trade-off process discussed earlier. Note that trade-offs can occur between two maintenance concepts, such as repair by dealers and repair by company-owned repair centers. There can be significant cost differences between the two concepts, and the choice of one can affect customer satisfaction and thereby sales.

As the ILS plan and its maintenance plan evolve, they are also subject to cost trade-off scrutiny. Formal methods for doing this are the level-of-repair analysis, the maintenance engineering analysis, quantitative and qualitative personnel requirements information, and the logistic support analysis.[6]

The level-of-repair analysis evaluates the cost of repairing an item at various maintenance levels (organizational, intermediate, or depot) so as to minimize cost and maximize availability. Programs are available for computer analysis, but an experienced maintainability engineer must still assemble the alternative approaches as input data and assess the meaning of the outputs.[7]

The maintenance engineering analysis usually includes a level-of-repair analysis and shows the resources needed and the reason for each maintenance action; summary sheets provide lists of the required resources. These summary output sheets are often arranged for convenient input to computer memories. In the computer, the data may be accessible to the LCC analyst for direct use in cost-estimating computer programs.

The quantitative and qualitative personnel requirements information is based on the maintenance engineering analysis. Each task is analyzed for the skill required, the number of people needed to do it, and the training required. The total number of people needed, their rank or pay grade, and their training are listed.

The logistic support analysis includes the maintenance engineering analysis, the level-of-repair analysis, and the personnel analysis and extends them to cover all support required, including operational matters. It also examines what directions must be given a system for various operations, the sequences of actions, and provisions such as fuel supply. This analysis, too, is often summarized for convenient use by computers and for cost analysis.

The division of the support work load between the military and civilian (mostly contractor) forces can affect LCC and certainly the accounts charged with the support costs. The development of the ILS plan should consider costs, military policy, and military capability in allocating work between military and civilian work forces.

Maintenance Costs

The maintenance work load depends on what must be done to prevent system failures, how often the system fails despite these efforts, and how expensive it is to repair. These system characteristics are quantitatively described by such words as *reliability, maintainability, durability, readiness,* and *availability.*

According to the standard military definition, *reliability* "is the probability that an item will perform its intended function for a specific interval under stated conditions."[8] Note that correct functioning, or conversely failure, remains to be defined; this can be crucial in measuring reliability. The failure rate (see Figure 4-2) is a commonly used measure of reliability. The reciprocal of the failure rate is called the mean time between failures (MTBF); this is not related to the life or durability of the item.

Maintainability is a characteristic of design and installation. It is expressed as the probability that an item will be

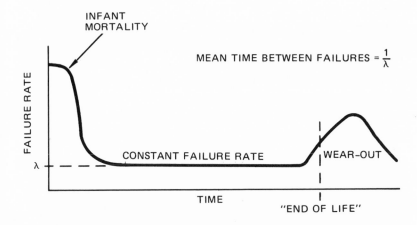

Figure 4-2. Reliability and Maintainability
Parameters

retained in or restored to a specified condition within a given period of time, provided that maintenance is performed in accordance with prescribed procedures and resources.[9] The maintenance location (organizational level, intermediate level, or depot) is implicit in the definition. Measures of maintainability are the mean time to repair (MTTR), the amount of active time it takes to restore an item to satisfactory operation after it has failed, and the mean down time (MDT), which is the sum of the MTTR, the logistics delay time (MLDT), and the administrative delay time (MADT). The MDT, therefore, includes the time required to obtain the parts, tools, personnel, and administrative paperwork and permission to proceed.

Availability is a measure of the proportion of time during which an item is capable of performing its function or operational mission.[10] Inherent availability (A_i) is the maximum theoretical availability of which the design is capable, without reference to a particular operational situation. Mathematically, inherent availability is expressed as:

$$A_i = \frac{\text{Up Time}}{\text{Up Time} + \text{Repair Time}} = \frac{\text{MTBF}}{\text{MTBF} + \text{MTTR}}$$

The operational availability (A_O) considers the logistic situation for an operation and is calculated as:

$$A_o = \frac{\text{Up Time}}{\text{Up Time} + \text{Down Time}} = \frac{\text{MTBF}}{\text{MTBF} + \text{MTTR} + \text{MLDT} + \text{MADT}}$$

Contracts often declare that availability is one of their preeminent requirements. A trade-off with LCC is occasionally suggested, implying that changes in availability can be given a dollar value (see Chapter 9).

Durability is usually used to mean the effective lifetime or wear-out life of the item. This is an imprecise term and should be avoided. Instead, it is better to define end of life in terms of LCC; that is, end of life occurs when continued use will increase the LCC. As a rough guage, the beginning of the wear-out rise in the failure rate (Figure 4-2) suggests that the end of life is near because maintenance costs are rising.

Readiness is the capability of a unit, ship, weapon system, or equipment to perform the missions or functions for which it has been organized or designed. The term may be used in a general sense or to express a level or degree of readiness.[11] Because the definition equivocates, *readiness* may be used in a number of senses. The preferred usage is as a measure of an entire organizational unit, including operating and maintenance manpower, supplies, and weapons. The quantitative measure of the readiness of an organization is then the proportion of time in which it is fully ready for combat operations.

Maintenance costs are a direct function of the characteristics discussed above. These measure how often an item fails (reliability, or failure rate), how long it takes to fix it (maintainability, or mean time to repair), and its resultant characteristics of availability, durability, and readiness. Because these measures determine support costs, many efforts have been made to control and enhance them. During R&D, the DOD has used contractual provisions for reliability and maintainability programs, with demonstrations, reliability improvement warranties (see Chapter 7), and extensive test programs, such as the "fly before buy" tests. Such efforts attempt to encourage design improvement of reliability, maintainability, and availability so as to reduce maintenance costs.

The cost-estimating relations given so far for maintenance costs are adequate for order-of-magnitude estimates but suffer from their inability to correlate with design characteristics. For LCC to be meaningful, it must be sensitive to design changes and must influence design. The process of trading design features for cost improvements is discussed in Chapter 9. In the past, logisticians and cost estimators often neglected the values estimated by the designers for reliability and maintainability; the values were often inaccurate and were couched in terms unfamiliar to logisticians and cost estimators. The assignment of logistic resources was done on the basis of preceding, similar systems and on the basis of the funds available. Now, LCC is encouraging a more analytical approach, and fortunately the quality of the reliability and maintainability estimates is improving.

Maintenance Levels

Maintenance is conducted at a number of levels. In the military, *organizational maintenance* is done by the operator or the personnel attached to the user organization. Although this maintenance is limited to simple operations, there is so much of it that the cost is large. *Intermediate maintenance* is carried out by the next higher echelon of support. The army includes direct support and general support in this category; the navy does this maintenance aboard tenders, or other large ships, such as carriers; the air force calls this "base maintenance." Intermediate maintenance uses more specialized personnel than organizational maintenance and needs more elaborate equipment, but it can be handled at fewer locations. Usually its cost is the smallest of the three levels. *Depot maintenance* is highly specialized, using skilled technicians for difficult repair and overhaul tasks. The few depots

are usually in the continental United States. Depot maintenance accounts for about a third of total maintenance costs,
even though centralized maintenance allows economies of
scale.

These proportions of costs are roughly in accordance with
general practice. As more work is assigned to intermediate
and depot levels, the volume increases and the cost of individual maintenance tasks decreases. Availability of the system
may also decline owing to the transit time required for parts
needing maintenance. Provision of adequate spares may improve availability but adds to costs. Selecting the trade-off
between cost and availability is the task of level-of-repair
analysis.

Note that the *mean time to repair* (MTTR), defined under
maintainability, must be separately determined for organizational repair actions, intermediate repair, and depot repair.
The total maintenance work load is the sum of the work
required to repair an item at each level at which it is handled.
Not all failed equipment is repaired. At each maintenance
level, some items are scrapped as more expensive to repair
than to replace. This proportion of scrapped items is an important maintenance cost parameter that cannot be generalized; it is a characteristic of the particular design.

Early in some programs, during the introduction of the
system into the service, contractor-augmented support is
sometimes used. That is, the contractor does some or all of
the maintenance while the service develops its own organized
maintenance capability. LCC analysis can be used to evaluate
the benefits of such augmented support efforts; scheduling
considerations, however, usually dominate the decision to use
or not to use contractor-augmented support.

Maintenance Personnel

To determine the cost of maintenance personnel, the
number of men required and their skill levels (pay grades)

must be evaluated. There are two general approaches to estimating the number of maintenance personnel. The first, which is essentially by analogy, adapts the number of maintenance personnel needed for a known system to the requirements of a new one. An example of this is the USAF CACE model in AFR 173-10.[12] This model is operationally oriented and is not well suited to guide design. Like other maintenance manpower estimates by analogy, it includes some unstated constraints. For example, doctrine may require that a maintenance capability be available twenty-four hours per day and further, for safety reasons, that at least two men must work together at all times. Manning a position on a round-the-clock basis requires at least five men for each position (allowing for weekends, vacations, sick leave, and so on), or ten men in all. This requirement is not influenced by the amount of work required, unless the work exceeds what two men, continuously available, can do. These manpower needs may increase if separate specialties are required, such as radar, electrical, ordnance, and automotive work.

The second approach uses a bottom up method, like the maintenance engineering analysis, and is sensitive to design characteristics. The failure rates of the system are multiplied by the repair time for each failure (or by an average repair time, MTTR) and by the annual operating hours of the system and the number of men required to do the repair. This provides the corrective maintenance man-hours per system. A similar evaluation of scheduled maintenance work load will give figures for the preventive maintenance man-hours needed. The sum of the two is the maintenance man-hours; if that figure is divided by the available productive man-hours per man-year (about 1,500 for most service billets), the number of men required can be obtained. This must be done separately for each level of maintenance. This bottom up method will give unrealistically low results, however, unless some corrective factors are applied. First, multiply the reliability failure rates by a factor of two or three to correct for those failures that are outside of reliability calculations. (Personnel errors, chain failures, use of equipment outside of specifications, and excessive environmental conditions cause failures that must be repaired, but these are not considered reliability failures.) The product is the rate of maintenance actions, as distinguished from the failure rate. Second, subtract the nonproductive time a repairman spends waiting for parts, tools, information, and authorizations from his time available for productive duty. Even with these corrections, the bottom up estimate is usually low. The use of test data, instead of analytically derived failure rates and repair times, improves the evaluation. Even with these corrections, some maintainability estimates have been as low as one-eighth of actual costs during initial deployment of new systems. Of course, repair time decreases with experience. Nevertheless, the fact that military maintenance is almost always more time-consuming than anticipated does not invalidate the usefulness of the LCC estimating process for the purpose of comparing alternatives. The bottom up method of calculating maintenance work load shows the real demands for manpower and is just as significant to the operational forces as the estimate by analogy. The analogy method is a useful way of estimating how many men to include on organizational charts. But military organizations (and many civilian ones, too) are chronically undermanned; if there is excess capacity in one area of the full organization chart, the extra men will be given other assignments. Thus, the reduced cost shown by the bottom up method of estimating is a real saving, either in money or in increased capability. The bottom up method of estimating maintenance manpower is, therefore, a valid design criterion.

After determining the number of personnel, it is necessary to specify their skill level (and pay grade). The "task and skill analysis" and the "quantitative and qualitative personnel requirements information" of the military services provide such information.[13] The analyst can estimate the cost of the given grades of personnel by using tables such as Table 4-1.

Provisioning

Provisioning costs are divided into *initial spares and repair parts, replacement spares and repair parts,* and *supply management.* The purchaser should procure initial spares at the same time as the production items, and their cost should be included in the purchase price. Spares that are separately ordered will usually cost more. The quantity of initial spares to order depends on how long it takes to reorder. If it takes, say, two years for the logistics system to recognize a need, order a replacement, receive it and transport it to where it is needed, then the initial order for spares must allow for at least two years of consumption. Few procurements purchase enough initial spares, for money spent on spares cannot buy more prime items. The shortsightedness of this approach is obvious to any operator whose system has been out of order due to lack of parts.

How many spares are needed for a two-year period? A simple percentage of 5 to 15 percent of the value of the operating system cost yields a rough first estimate. Predominately dormant systems would use the lower value, and high-use systems the larger value. A more precise answer uses the system failure rates and operating time and calculates specific values. Note that the system failure rates must be corrected, as was done for the maintenance work load calculations. Reliability-based predictions of the need for spares, however, have often been even less satisfactory than reliability predictions of maintenance needs. The critical question for provisioning is often "What specific items will be the most troublesome and be chronically in short supply?" A recent study has stated that reliability predictions are often too uncertain to be used as a basis for spares provisioning.[14] Provisioning decisions have to cope with the fact that the shortage of a single part may make it impossible to operate a piece of equipment, whereas errors in maintenance work load predictions can be averaged over the system as a whole. The reliability effort during development tries to eliminate each of the troublesome items from design. After deployment, the items with unusually high failure rates and high provisioning demand are precisely those that the reliability program did *not* discover and correct. But the LCC analyst need not have the jaundiced view of reliability data that provisioning personnel may develop. The cost estimates inherently have the same averaging effect as the maintenance work load estimates, and so reliability-based calculations *are* useful for LCC.

Provisioning allowance lists, showing the range and depth of spares, can be drawn up based on the corrected reliability estimates. These allowance lists should be based on the desired availability of the system, because the logistic delay time (MLDT) depends on what proportion of spares is kept at organization level and what is held at more remote locations. These values can be obtained from the logistics plan, examined for their consequences, and modified if necessary. Here, again, LCC analysis interacts with the various program plans. These plans are needed for the LCC analysis, and the LCC analysis refines them.

Spares are stocked at the organization, intermediate, and depot levels, with replenishment stocks available at more remote locations. The requirements for replenishment stocks are usually determined by experience and judgment because the analytical procedure for determining the number of spares required for a specified availability at more than two levels is quite complex (practically impossible). The procedure includes determination of the expected back-order rate (the proportion of orders that cannot be filled on demand) using the availability or readiness requirements. A range of 1 percent to 5 percent is usual for the back-order rate.[15]

The cost of replacement spares is determined in much the same way as that of initial spares. For early estimates, use the same method and data, with one exception. Replacement spares will be procured, for the most part, after production has been completed. Costs for these additional procurements can be significantly higher and should be anticipated. The use of optimal economic ordering quantities analysis can control these costs to some extent, usually by buying large quantities at a time.[16] Because there is a fixed cost for every order, small quantities effectively cost the buyer more per unit than large quantities. The quantity discounts offered by many suppliers increase this effect and encourage larger quantity orders. However, it also costs money in lost interest, warehouse space, and so on to hold supplies in inventory. The optimum balance between these two cost effects is the economic order quantity.

Reliability and end-of-life are ultimately the most influential factors in provisioning costs. During design, the cost of improvements in reliability to decrease the need for spares should be balanced against the savings in the cost of spares. This process can be highly speculative. Once the system is in operation, however, more dependable data are available on the usage of spare parts. A systematic study to determine which spares are most used and the cost of improving their reliability has often proved profitable. The U.S. Air Force PRAM program has shown rates of return of as high as 250 times the investment.[17]

Another cost of provisioning is the management of supply. This is usually separated into the administrative cost of entering a new item into the supply system, and the cost of retaining each item in the supply system. Great variability exists in the estimation of these costs. Estimates of the cost of entering an item have ranged from $25 to $1,000 per year. The higher values are probably correct in that they approximate the total cost of the supply system apportioned among all items.[18]

The analyst should evaluate how much provisioning paperwork costs the contractor. The military services have elaborate and expensive systems for ordering and controlling supplies, in addition to the item entry and retainment costs. The contractor's costs are usually estimated on the basis of the number of line entries.

As part of the review of the ILS plan, the analyst should consider the trade-offs involved in pre-positioned stocks and rotatable pools of material. Supply concepts such as these must be examined with the provisioning specialists to get minimum LCC estimates.

Support Equipment

The tools, test equipment, trucks, generators, workstands, and calibration apparatus needed to operate and maintain a weapon system constitute its support equipment. They are usually categorized as either *peculiar support equipment* (for that weapon system only) or *common support equipment* (catalog items already in the inventory and in use by the service). The list of support equipment is part of the ILS plan and is generated and refined by the maintenance engineering analysis and the logistic support analysis. Cost trade-offs may be a part of this process, with the participation of the LCC analyst. The amount of support equipment needed depends on the maintenance concept and the reliability of the system.

Support equipment is usually a cost driver and may account for 10 percent to 50 percent of the cost of the prime equipment. The significant trade-off is the choice between placement of support equipment at the user level for fast repair and high availability or placement at more remote locations, using fewer equipments with more skilled personnel, for cheaper repair but a lower availability due to the longer turnaround time. This trade-off is one of those done during the level-of-repair analysis.[19]

The cost of the peculiar support equipment is estimated in the same way as that of other manufactured or purchased equipment, though at lower production rates. Common support equipment costs can usually be found in catalogs.[20] In addition, the cost of supporting the support equipment should not be overlooked.

Software Maintenance

The need to revise and correct computer programming software is commonly called software maintenance. Purists will claim that the original programming of the computer has not changed in the sense of having degraded or failed, although changes may be desired or latent defects may have been discovered. This is not just a semantic problem, because the nature of the changes desired or made determines whether the cost of modification is categorized as maintenance or system improvement. The correction of latent defects is truly maintenance; other software changes should be in the system improvement category. In any case, revising the programming is a major and expensive task. One naval system uses more than 300 full-time programmers to keep its software operational.

A simple CER for software maintenance is:

Maintenance cost = (Number of instructions to be changed per month) x (Cost per man-month) x (3)/(Difficulty constant)

The difficulty constant is found in Table 2-2. Or, estimates by analogy may be used. A more complete discussion of software maintenance is in Chapter 8.

Testing Policy

The ILS plan will usually state the operational testing policy for the weapon. Is there periodic operability testing? How frequent and how thorough is it? Is the test equipment built into the weapon or is external, portable equipment used? Each of these questions will significantly influence maintenance costs and should be examined by the LCC analyst. Generally, tests seek both to improve the weapon's reliability and to engender confidence in the user. The latter purpose is not costable and is expensive. Most decisions about testing based on cost considerations alone will seek to minimize testing. The testing mystique is powerful, however, and tends to counteract cost pressures.

Maintenance Computer Models

The U.S. Air Force Logistic Command has developed a series of logistic support cost models. These use ten equations for provisioning, on-equipment maintenance labor, off-equipment maintenance labor, inventory entry and supply management, support equipment, personnel training and training equipment, management and technical data, software acquisition and support, fuel, and engine replacement. The models have been adapted for aircraft, electronics and meteorological equipment, and others. They provide an orderly framework for the calculation of these costs and relieve the analyst of some of the tedious repetitive calculations, but they are not a substitute for thinking out the entire costing problem. These models and others are discussed in detail in Chapter 8.

Training

School training is costed as a separate part of operations and maintenance, but unit training is costed under the general operations of the unit. Schools during the R&D phase are usually conducted by the prime contractor and located at that plant. During the investment (deployment) phase, the service schools start. The LCC analyst should only cost schooling peculiar to the weapon system. Basic training and general training, e.g., electronics, are costed as part of personnel billet costs.

A training plan is needed for cost estimating. This plan, like the others, should say what is to be done and provide a schedule in sufficient detail to use as a basis for a cost estimate. Training by a contractor, as well as by various service schools, should be considered. The cost estimate can then serve as the basis for evaluating the various options, thus continuing the optimization process. One possible trade-off is the combination of test operations with schooling; the students run tests and learn by doing. Combining the two may reduce initial costs but lengthen schedules; perhaps the quality of the schooling may be degraded to accommodate the testing requirements, or vice versa. The dialectic process between the cost estimate and the training plan will refine both.

Training equipment and facilities. This category includes all of the training aids used by instructors and students. Simulators, mock-ups, books, manuals, special buildings, and any other related equipment should be costed. Classrooms and standard buildings are usually not charged because the expenditure is not for a particular weapon system. The cost of this training equipment is estimated in the same way as that of other manufactured items, although quantities will usually be smaller. To obviate the need for specially designed training equipment, the use of test equipment setups or of operational equipment for training should be considered. Training equipment and facilities costs are usually part of the investment phase; often their design is postponed until that phase.

Training services. The cost of instructors is the primary training service cost. Their preparation time, as well as instruction time, is included. On a calendar basis, the preparation of classroom material takes most instructors at least twice as much time as instruction itself. That is, the instructor will need four weeks of full-time preparation to teach a class that runs for two weeks, even if the class is only six hours per day. The cost of training services can be approximated at $60,000 per year for contractor instructors, and Table 4-1 can be used for military instructors with travel time and expenses added.

Trainees' time. The number of trainees, their pay grade, and the length of time they are in school are the factors in schooling cost. Some attrition should be expected during schooling; 10 percent to 15 percent more trainees should be recruited than graduates are needed. Travel time and expense should be added to the cost of the trainees' pay and allowances.

The number of graduates needed depends on force requirements plus replacements for turnover. The annual military turnover rates are typically 40 to 50 percent for enlisted personnel and 10 percent for officers and civilians.[21]

Technical Manuals

The technical manuals and other logistic data for operation and maintenance are vital to an economical system. The ILS plan will include a list of the manuals to be used and a schedule for their preparation, publication, and distribution. This schedule is particularly important because the manuals cannot be written until the design has been completed, although they are needed for training operations before the first deliveries of equipment for customer test operations. Manuals are therefore a pacing item (a "critical path," in PERT language). All costing of manuals should consider this very demanding schedule constraint typical of new weapon systems. A generous overtime allowance is appropriate.

Early estimates of manual preparation costs are based on a CER using a standard cost per page, from $250 per page to $1,000 per page, depending on the difficulty of the material and the type of manual. This covers the research needed to write the manuals and the cost of preparing illustrations and camera-ready copy. As more detailed information becomes available, better cost estimates can be made (by analogy, by detail CERs, by industrial engineering methods). Some manual pages, such as those illustrating assembly procedures, can cost considerably more than a page of text.[22]

The level of detail required in the manual, and hence its length, is a function of the maintenance concept. If only a few large parts of the system are removed on failure, discarded, and replaced, the manuals and the maintenance task they describe are simple, short, and cheap. If many small modules are removed on failure, replaced, and then repaired, the need for manuals and maintenance personnel increases. Another cost trade-off may be needed to balance the level of repair with the consequent costs for manuals, provisioning, and so on.

The cost of preparing manuals may be a part of the engineering development process and charged to the R&D phase, or preparation may be separately funded later as part of the investment phase. Ordinarily, the customer prints, binds, and distributes manuals as part of the investment phase. These costs are estimated on the basis of the number of pages and the number of copies, such as $0.10 per page per copy. Lastly, the maintenance of the manuals during the life of the system must be estimated. Here again, the first estimates use a cost per page per year, such as $55. This should cover all research, writing, and administrative costs necessary for maintaining the manuals. Revised editions can be costed on the basis of the number of pages to be changed; these new pages cost whatever the original pages cost.

Site Preparation and Installation

A separate, identifiable cost is the expense of preparing the site for the system and the effort to install the system. Most site preparation costs can be handled as construction costs (see Chapter 5). Occasionally, site preparation costs are strictly military costs, as in the case of troops used to clear and level a site for an artillery battery.

Installation costs for ground systems are essentially a part of the site preparation costs. For aircraft and ship systems, however, the installation costs are a much larger problem.

Particularly careful estimates should be prepared for ship systems, where installation costs can constitute half the purchase price. The costs involved in rip-out of existing equipment, preparing foundations, and providing plumbing, electrical power, signal wiring, chilled water, air conditioning, and communications require close consideration. Aircraft installations have similar problems, though they are not usually so complex. The services of a marine estimator are a valuable asset.

Security Requirements

Many military systems require special security measures. These may be simply fences, gates, vaults, bunkers or other passive devices, or a guard patrol or intrusion detection devices may be necessary. In some cases, the security requirements may include tanks, aircraft, or ships. These clearly involve some additional costs that must be included. The services' planning references are of great help in pricing these security measures.[23]

O&S Data Sources

As in previous estimating procedures, O&S cost estimating should be based on data drawn from experience. Available data will usually need to be interpreted, analyzed, collated, and transformed to be usable. Most contractors of military equipment have such data on their own equipments, though often less than complete. Contractor data usually cover the engineering models or early operational models. Data on failure rates and repair costs need to be modified for maturation of the equipment and personnel; this tends to decrease failure rates, repair times, and therefore maintenance costs. On the other hand, later field experience will involve personnel with less motivation and training, which may increase failure rates and repair times. Studies have shown that the repair time measured in factory demonstrations, for example, can increase by two to eight times in operational experience.

Each of the three military services has published some cost data. The air force manual is extensive and most useful for LCC purposes; it includes two simple LCC models for aircraft and missiles. The army handbook and the navy manual are designed more for force planning work within the services than for LCC estimates; nevertheless, both contain a wealth of information that can be used with careful analysis.[24]

The air force has a logistic data gathering system designated as 66-1, and the navy has a similar system designated as the maintenance and material management system. In both of these, records of maintenance data are suitable for automated data processing so as to provide management control over costs. Neither system will provide failure rates, repair times, maintenance costs, or provisioning costs at the equipment level; all these costs are included but are aggregated at higher levels. With care, both sources can be analyzed to disaggregate the data. The methods for such analysis vary greatly, depending on the specific equipment of interest and the current configuration of the data systems. As suggested earlier, it is often expedient to go directly to operating units to obtain O&S data or to learn how to disaggregate the service's large data collection system.

J. R. Nelson criticizes "the lack of disaggregated, homogeneous, longitudinal ownership data."[25] The DOD has been trying for several years to gather better data.[26] A recent DOD handbook is a strong attempt to provide better data; it deals with such issues as the distinction between direct and indirect costs, and between maintenance costs and modification costs.[27] The problem of accounting for depot costs is complex and will not soon be resolved, but the data are there. The services are moving toward improved management information systems.[28] Although a determined analyst now requires time, intelligence, and ingenuity to extract the needed information, easier times lie ahead.

Work Breakdown Structure

The WBS (see Table 2-3) is the standard military frame-work for the costs discussed in this book. In simple analyses, the WBS works well, but it has a number of inadequacies for LCC. For example, operating costs have no place in the WBS framework, except possibly at level 1, which is much too highly aggregated a level to permit an understanding of their makeup. Maintenance costs, on the other hand, can be conveniently charged to the various hardware elements at level 3 or below. Some training costs can be segregated at level 3, but there is no convenient place to list trainees' time charges. Provisioning for initial spares and repair parts is shown at level 2, but there is no descriptive WBS category for replacement spares. Software maintenance costs do not have a proper WBS location. In short, many O&S costs do not readily fit into the WBS. A more capacious system is needed.

Matrix Presentation

A matrix presentation is the best solution to the problem of providing more categories for cost elements. A new set of cost categories accommodates and emphasizes the costing methods used in military budgeting; it is a cost-breakdown structure (CBS), as in Table 4-2, and appears in Figure 4-3 as the vertical axis, specifying the content of each row. The CBS categorizes costs according to the function performed, rather than by the part of the hardware affected. Note functions in Table 4-2 such as "acquisition," "supply support," and "program management"; note also that the separation of acquisition into hardware categories such as "prime equipment," "support equipment," and "test equipment" tends to blur this categorization by function. Just as the WBS is not a pure hardware breakdown, neither is the CBS a purely functional breakdown. The WBS is retained across the top of Figure 4-3 as the horizontal axis, specifying the components

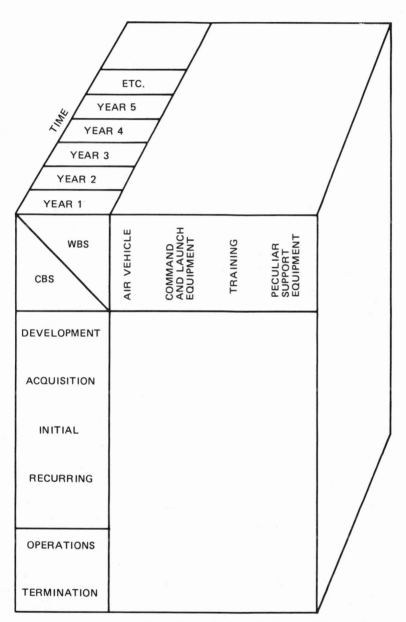

Figure 4-3. A Cost Matrix Provides Additional
Cost Elements

Table 4-2
COST BREAKDOWN STRUCTURE

DEVELOPMENT	INITIAL
Prime Contractor	Technical Data
Other Contractor	Acquisition
Government	Reproduction and Distribution
Training	First Year Maintenance
Pay and Allowances	Revision
Facilities	Training
Prototype Testing	Pay and Allowances
Test Site	Travel
Modification	Contractor Support
Installation of Prototype System	Aids
Operation of Test Site	Acquisition
Restoration	Installation
Pay and Allowances	Supply Support
Travel	Acquisition of Initial Spares
Transportation of Material	Introduction Into the Supply System
Program Management	New FSN's in Prime System
ACQUISITION	New FSN's in Support Equipment
Acquisition of Prime System	
Acquisition of Support Equipment	
Acquisition of Test Equipment	

Table 4-2 (Continued)

RECURRING
Prime System
  Transportation to Installation Site
  Installation
  Technical Data Maintenance
Supply Support
  FSN Maintenance
    Prime System
    Support Equipment
  Acquisition of Replenishment Spares
Training
  Pay and Allowances (Navy Personnel)
  Course material
  Course Fee
Management
Maintenance
  Labor
    Organizational (Replace)
    Intermediate (Repair)
    Depot

Repair Material
  Intermediate
  Depot
Transportation and Packaging
  Shipping
  Packaging Material
  Material Handling Labor
Preventive Maintenance
Facilities
  Shop Space
    O/I Level
    Depot Level
  Inventory Storage
    O/I Level
    Depot Level
OPERATIONS
Personnel Pay and Allowances
Facility Space
Electric Power
TERMINATION
Salvage
Transportation

of each column. These two structures—the CBS and the WBS —are not truly orthogonal,[29] and therefore some of the intersections (cells) will usually show zeros in the operational/ site activation column of the WBS.

A third dimension of the matrix can be used for time, usually in years, quarters, or months. This, again, greatly increases the number of cost categories available, allowing more specificity in designating costs and in ways of recovering the cost data. This new dimension also is not orthogonal with the other two. The CBS sequence of phases is roughly a time sequence so that the latter phases of the CBS will always be empty for the beginning of the time dimension and so that the beginning of the CBS dimension (R&D) will usually be empty for the end of the time dimension. Because the CBS phases of an actual program may overlap or have intervening gaps, the timed presentation can be helpful in clarifying the flow of money. This annual funding requirement for a program is always needed for budgeting and appropriations.

The matrix presentation is widely used because it allows great flexibility and convenience in presenting LCC data. The matrix structure also provides a checklist to ensure that no item of cost has been overlooked.

O&S Estimating Procedure

Before systematically examining all of the costs discussed above, see whether any cost drivers have been omitted. Does one of the alternatives have a larger attrition rate? Can this be quantified in money costs? Does an alternative require the use of a particular manpower skill that is unavailable? Can this shortage be quantified in money? After completing such an intuitive, exploratory check, then consider each of the major costs.

1. *Personnel.* Estimate the number and cost of operators and maintenance men at each level of maintenance, full-time or on demand. Use billet costs with fringe costs to develop

manpower cost.

2. *Support equipment.* Compile a list of operations and maintenance at each level. Estimate costs by analogy or CERs.

3. *Provisioning.* Use the rough rules of thumb for the first estimate. The second time, use CERs that are sensitive to design reliability and maintainability values; the referenced computer models are most convenient.

4. *Maintenance.* Estimate those personnel not included in (1). Estimate the provisioning not included in (3). Usually these people will be involved in depot or factory-level maintenance.

5. *Cost improvements.* Problems with the ILS plan, the maintenance concept, and the major design cost drivers should be apparent from the first four steps. Solve these problems.

6. *Complete O&S model.* Prepare a complete O&S cost estimate, including transportation, training, manuals, and so on, and revise the top four categories on the basis of the cost-improvement changes.

Notes

1. U.S. Air Force, *USAF Cost and Planning Factors,* AFR 173-10, vols. 1, 2 (Washington, D.C.: Department of the Air Force, 1977); U.S. Navy, *Navy Program Factors Manual,* OPNAV 90P-02, vols. 1, 2 (Philadelphia: Naval Publications and Forms Center, 1977); U.S. Army, Comptroller of the Army, Directorate of Cost Analysis, *Army Force Planning Cost Handbook* (Washington, D.C.: Department of the Army, 1977).

2. Ibid.

3. U.S. Army, General Material and Supply Activity, *Quarterly Supply Information Letter* (New Cumberland Army Depot, Pa.: General Material and Supply Activity, 1978).

4. See note 1.

5. U.S. Department of Defense, *Development of Integrated Logistic Support for Systems/Equipment*, Directive 4100.35 (Washington, D.C.: Department of Defense, 1976).

6. U.S. Department of Defense, *Logistic Support Analysis*, MIL-STD-1388-1 and -2 (Washington, D.C.: Department of Defense, 1973); U.S. Department of Defense, *Contract Training Programs*, MIL-STD-1379 (Washington, D.C.: Department of Defense, 1976), a standard that provides a guide to all DOD personnel and skills analyses; U.S. Army, *ILS Maintenance Engineering Analysis Data*, TM 38-703-3 (Washington, D.C.: Department of the Army, 1969).

7. U.S. Navy, Naval Weapons Engineering Support Activity, *Level of Repair: Users Training Manual*, ESA-75 (Washington, D.C.: Naval Weapons Engineering Support Activity, 1973).

8. U.S. Department of Defense, *Definitions of Effectiveness Terms for Reliability, Maintainability, Human Factors, and Safety*, MIL-STD-721 (Washington, D.C.: Department of Defense, 1970).

9. Ibid.

10. Ibid.

11. U.S. Army, *Unit Readiness Reporting*, AR 220-1 (Washington, D.C.: Department of Defense, 1975).

12. See note 1.

13. See note 6.

14. James H. Brady, "The Utility of Reliability Predictions for Logistics Forecasting," *Logistics Spectrum*, Summer 1977.

15. Bruce Hoadley and Daniel P. Heyman, *A Two Echelon Inventory Model with Purchases, Dispositions, Shipments, Returns, and Transshipments* (Holmdell, N.J.: Bell Telephone Laboratories, 1976).

16. Eugene L. Grant and W. Grant Ireson, *Principles of Engineering Economy* (New York: Ronald Press, 1970).

17. Grant E. Gabel, "Capitalizing on Cost-Reducing Op-

portunities," *Defense Management Journal,* January 1977.

18. National Security Industrial Association, Maintenance Advisory Committee, Spares Provisioning Panel, *Annual Cost of Keeping a Repair Part in the Supply System* (Washington, D.C., 1968). At the time, a high-activity item's annual cost was estimated at $4,400 and a low-activity item's at $140.

19. See note 6.

20. U.S. Army, *Supply Bulletin* 700-20 (Chambersburg, Pa.: U.S. Army Depot Command, 1977).

21. See note 1.

22. U.S. Navy, *Government Managers Technical Manual Cost Analysis Guide* (Philadelphia: Naval Air Technical Services Facility, 1970).

23. See note 1.

24. Ibid.

25. J. P. Nelson, *Life Cycle Analysis of Aircraft Turbine Engines: Executive Summary,* R-2103/1-AF (Santa Monica, Calif.: Rand Corp., 1977).

26. John R. Jivatode, "Tracking the Costs of Depot Maintenance," *Defense Management Journal,* July 1977.

27. U.S. Department of Defense, *DOD Depot Maintenance Support Accounting and Production Reporting Handbook* (Washington, D.C.: Department of Defense, 1977).

28. U.S. Navy, *Visibility and Management of Support Costs—Ships* (Washington, D.C.: Chief of Naval Operations, 1976).

29. *Orthogonal:* a term from vector algebra meaning that the scalar product of the two vectors is zero, because the angle between them is 90 degrees. In the sense used here, the 90-degree angle between two dimensions (axes) would mean that movement along one dimension has no effect along the other dimension. For the cost-breakdown structure shown, however, movement along that dimension is also movement along the time dimension, and therefore the two dimensions are not orthogonal. H. B. Phillips, *Vector Algebra* (New York: Wiley, 1933).

5
Miscellaneous Costs and Revenue

Most programs incur costs for new or modified construction. In some instances, the cost differences between alternative programs may be significant; in other cases, the very magnitude of construction costs is of interest. In both situations, construction costs should be estimated at the beginning and followed progressively with more detailed estimates throughout the life cycle of the program.

Disposing of an item at the end of its life can also be expensive. Nuclear waste is the most notorious example. Offsetting credits may be obtained from the salvage price of parts of the item. Other miscellaneous expenditures may be required by the Energy Research and Development Agency (ERDA), the Environmental Protection Agency (EPA), and the Veterans Administration (VA).

Construction Costs

Military construction may include a wide variety of facilities for operations, maintenance, training, and supply. Warehouses, barracks, missile silos, test ranges, launch pads, airfields, wharves, roads, bridges, pipelines, and depots may be needed. Nonmilitary projects may require similar construction. For LCC purposes, the cost of conventional facilities, such as additional barracks, offices, airfields, and other common facilities, is of small importance. These expenses are frequently factored into the CERs for manpower or logistics costs. The more important forms of construction for LCC purposes are novel items, such as new mobile missile silos, launch pads, test range modifications, or other special weapon-system facilities. These are the cost drivers to examine in comparing alternative systems. Thus, the LCC analyst will perennially struggle with the costs of constructing unusual facilities rather than those of conventional work. The help of an expert facilities estimator can make a significant difference to the LCC analyst seeking to cost these unusual tasks. The LCC analyst should be cautious about making even rough, order-of-magnitude construction estimates without expert advice. Although facilities estimators have the uncomfortable habit of asking many detailed questions to which there are as yet no answers and are slow in making even a rough guess, the intricacies of construction estimating justify their caution. If the LCC analyst must produce some figures, current costs can be obtained from various estimating guides.[1]

Estimating Methods

The same three familiar methods are used for construction costs as were used for R&D, production, and operating and support costs.

Analogy. Use the analogy method during the early phases of the program when a rough, order-of-magnitude estimate will suffice. The method is the same as before. Segment the task until the parts can be seen as similar to past tasks; then analyze the differences between these parts and the past tasks and estimate the cost impact of these differences. Among the new factors that might modify construction costs are geographical differences. For example, because the water table at Cape Canaveral lies close to the surface, foundation costs there are higher than at Vandenberg Air Force Base. Material and labor costs differ in various parts of the country and may be much higher in inaccessible locations, such as mountains and islands, than at more central locations. More-over, a sudden increase in labor demand due to military construction can seriously distort wage patterns. Inhospitable climatic conditions will also raise costs. The analyst should consider all of these factors in estimating by analogy and should modify the estimate accordingly. If the impact of these circumstances is unknown, state this in the ground rules and assumptions accompanying the estimate.

Cost-estimating relations. The construction industry has many CERs for conventional facilities. Home construction costs are commonly estimated at $50 per square foot of floor area. The construction of factory buildings costs at least $100 per square foot.[2] Most of these CERs will be of little help to the LCC analyst because, almost by definition, they are not available for novel construction. Again, the standard remedy is to segment the facility into familiar parts that can be estimated, although this may require more detailed descriptions than are available. Consider the LCC analyst who was first confronted with the need to estimate the cost of testing nuclear weapons or of building missile silos. He must have searched hard for familiar parts to estimate. Some gross CERs, such as those based on cubic yards of concrete or tons of structural steel used, might have provided a helpful start for an educated guess.

Industrial engineering estimates. The detailed industrial engineering estimate process requires a description of the required construction and of the site, along with a schedule. The work of the various specialties, such as masonry, carpentry, pilings, concrete, mechanical, and electrical, must be planned. Each of these is then separately estimated, at whatever level of detail is appropriate. Such estimates should be made by facilities estimating specialists, or requested as bids from contractors. Such estimates are accurate to within 5 to 10 percent of final costs. The drawback to this approach is that it requires a mass of detailed information and a good deal of time.

Rental Costs

Rental of existing facilities is an alternative to the construction of new ones. Because monthly rental costs are apt to be about 1 percent of the purchase (construction) price, rental can save money on short-term programs of less than 100 months. About half of the rent, however, goes for interest and taxes. Government construction and ownership lower interest rates, and government-owned facilities pay no taxes. It may therefore be cost-effective for the government to build new facilities, even for programs of less than 100 months, particularly if a significant salvage price seems possible.

Facilities Contracts

Some contractors operate in government-owned facilities, which are often furnished rent-free for use on government contracts, under a *facility contract*. In comparing the costs of material from these contractors with that charged by contractors using their own facility, LCC estimators routinely add an equivalent rent to the first contractor's bid, but it is rarely a significant amount—about 1 percent.

Transportation Costs

The cost of transportation of material and personnel is occasionally significant in LCC. In the case of known itineraries, such costs are usually estimated on a ton-mile basis. In the case of overseas shipment to unknown destinations, a gross estimate of $2 per pound is used. These estimates will need to be refined in several ways as more information becomes available. Insurance costs should be separately delineated. There is, as another example, a distinction between first destination (the point of delivery to the customer) and second destination (usually the first active-duty station for equipment). Another term used is *permanent change of station*—the accumulated costs of military personnel traveling between assignments. A CER is available for each military service based on rotation rates, location, and rank.

For exact transportation costs, consult specialists. The intricacies of these costs overwhelm other estimators.

Modification Programs

A common LCC task is a comparison between the cost of modifying an existing system and the cost of developing a new one. Previous chapters have provided methods for estimating the costs of a new system. The cost of modifying a system is estimated in essentially similar ways, except that the analyst must decide how to handle the cost of the existing equipment to be used in the modified configuration. What costs are relevant, and which are to be ignored as "sunk costs"?

Sunk Costs

The cost of equipment already built or for which funds are irrevocably committed should be considered as sunk costs and not as part of the investment for the modified program. If the equipment must be replaced, however, the LCC analyst should add the replacement costs to the cost of the modified configuration. Similarly, if support equipment is used for the modified configuration, and if these support items must be replaced in the inventory, then the cost of the replacement items must be carried in the investment phase of the LCC.

These are not clear-cut decisions, because it is not always clear whether an item will be replaced. For example, a proposed program considered the use of an existing ICBM as part of a new weapon system. If some of these missiles were withdrawn from the inventory, would they be replaced or would the air force want to buy new, different missiles to replace the old ones? Did the proposed program provide a convenient reason for buying new, improved missiles? The analyst must decide, make his decision clear in the ground rules, and proceed. Higher authorities can subsequently judge and rule.

Operating and Support Costs of Modified Systems

The costs of modified systems are much easier to estimate than those of new systems. Past history is available and should be used. The usual CERs for O&S costs may require some modification. For example, provisioning costs for spares are estimated in the basis of the procurement price of the basic item. When the basic item has been extensively modified, neither the original cost, nor the sum of the original cost and the modification cost, nor the modification cost alone is applicable. A new basis for the CER for spares must be developed. The sum of the original cost of the residual portion plus the modification costs for new equipment (not for removal work) is a good first approximation. Compare these results with previous history for reasonableness.

The maintenance and reliability characteristics of older equipment will certainly differ from those of new equipment. Ask reliability and maintainability specialists about the effect of the modification on these characteristics. Be careful of the routine claims that the new equipment has improved design characteristics with better reliability and maintainability; it often does not work out that way.

Disposal Costs

For most weapon systems, disposal costs are small, compared to other costs incurred. There are exceptions, though. Although it is possible to detonate small munitions, larger explosive devices, particularly nuclear devices, may be troublesome to destroy. The U.S. Air Force spent years trying to dispose of large stocks of Agent Orange herbicide after the Vietnam War. It may be very expensive to destroy missile silos, bomb shelters, and similar large concrete structures, and public opinion may not countenance abandonment of these structures intact. A plan should be prepared, albeit brief, at the early stages of the program. This plan can then be costed, beginning the trade-off process between the plan and the cost analysis. Early consideration of the disposal problem can prevent later embarrassment and assure a complete LCC estimate.

Salvage Revenue

After a weapon system has been demilitarized, some portions of it can usually be sold. Ships and other large iron or steel structures are often worth a substantial amount for scrap. Salvage revenue usually consists of scrap prices less dismantling and demilitarizing costs. Recent changes affecting legal liability for accidents or damage caused during dismantling operations have significantly increased insurance costs and thereby decreased salvage revenues. Rough estimates or complete bids can be obtained from dismantling, wrecking, or scrap firms.

The difference between disposal costs and salvage price is listed as a fourth phase (after R&D, investment, and O&S) of the program life cycle. Some LCC models include these as negative values in the investment phase, but this is not recommended because it blurs the meaning of "investment."

Because disposal and salvage costs lie far in the future

when the initial LCC estimate is made, most people regard them as less important than present costs. The method of evaluating the reduced importance of future costs in comparison to present costs is known as *discounting* and will be discussed in Chapter 6.

Energy Research and Development Agency

The Energy Research and Development Agency may contribute to LCC by requiring (1) additional efforts to reduce fuel consumption and (2) special efforts to reduce the effects of nuclear energy on personnel and equipment. The costs of reducing fuel consumption are primarily R&D costs, with perhaps some change in the production costs of modified engines or carburetors; these costs are balanced by fuel cost savings and may result in overall economies.

Cost may be incurred during R&D and during production to reduce the effects of nuclear radiation. These may range from the shielding of nuclear power plants to protective equipment for crew members during nuclear explosions and should not present any novel cost-estimating problems. The U.S. Army requires that ERDA costs be separately presented in LCC estimates.[3] Other services do not ask for separate calculations, nor should they be volunteered.

Environmental Protection Agency

Increasing public pressure is being placed on the military forces and on all governmental agencies to lessen the impact of new equipment on the environment, especially during peacetime. This can result in significant R&D, investment, O&S, and disposal costs.

The environmental requirements vary from the control of sewage effluents on navy ships to an almost complete moratorium on chemical, bacteriological, and radiological weapons. The cost-estimating procedures for such requirements follow the method outlined in previous chapters. Unless the purpose is to highlight the impact of a particular regulation, however, the costs of environmental protection should not be segregated. Environmental protection costs should be included as part of all other costs.

Veterans' Benefits

Because Veterans Administration funds are separately appropriated by the Congress and are not available to the DOD, their cost is not usually included in Defense Department LCC estimates. Nevertheless, veterans' benefits cost about $4,000 to $6,000 per man-year for active military personnel and correspond to the pensions, life insurance plans, and other benefits for which private contractors charge in their overhead rates. Furthermore, unlike the private contractor, the military does not charge for a number of its overhead functions, such as headquarters staff and executive offices. On the other hand, the civilian contractor benefits from various government subsidies, such as tax incentives, protective tariffs, and research services. Thus, military-civilian cost differences may be significant in comparisons between programs having widely different manpower requirements. Note that all of the costs discussed above are usually relatively small, uncertain, and subject to dispute and can reasonably be omitted. The analyst should limit the scope of LCC estimates to the incremental costs clearly assignable to a particular project and should make sure that such costs can be included in the relevant accounting systems. The omission of such costs as veterans' benefits should be stated in the ground rules.

Foreign Military Sales

LCC estimates involving sales of products overseas have

novel considerations. Particularly complex are military sales involving coproduction with foreign partners. Facts that should be considered are:

1. Currency exchange fluctuations: pegged or floating; barter arrangements.

2. Allocation of nonrecurring costs among participating organizations.

3. Technology transfer and associated costs.

4. Economic escalation indices (inflation-deflation) for each country.

5. Labor rates, fringe benefits, and union policies (such as layoff and retirement) vary from country to country, and CERs must be adjusted.

6. Different accounting systems may make it impossible to compare overhead rates.

7. Transportation costs may be much higher than usual.

8. Procurement and costing policies of each procuring country may be different; the U.S. DOD Armed Services Procurement Regulations may not apply.

Notes

1. *Current Construction Costs* (Walnut Creek, Calif.: Lee Saylor, 1977); *Light Construction Estimating and Engineering Standards* (Solana Beach, Calif.: Richardson Engineering Services, 1977); *General Construction Estimating Standards* (Solana Beach, Calif.: Richardson Engineering Services, 1977); *Building Construction Cost Data* (Duxbury, Mass.: Robert Snow Means Co., 1977); F. C. Jelen, *Cost and Optimization Engineering* (New York: McGraw-Hill, for the American Association of Cost Engineers, 1970); U.S. Army, *Staff Officers' Field Manual, Organizational, Technical, and Logistics Data* (Washington, D.C.: Department of the Army, 1976).

2. See the sources in note 1 for other CERs.

3. U.S. Army, *Standards for Presentation and Documentation of Life Cycle Cost Estimates for Army Material Systems,* Pamphlet no. 11-5 (Washington, D.C.: Department of the Army, 1976).

6
Inflation and Discounting

The preceding chapters have provided the basis for cost estimating. Subsequent chapters will discuss what to do with these estimates, how they are used for design decisions, and how to manage a program effectively with them. This chapter will focus on the effects of time on the cost estimates.

Both inflation and discounting modify the relation of future costs to initial costs. These analytical techniques influence the central idea of LCC, procurement on the basis of total costs.

Inflation

In recent years, monetary inflation has been a continuous worldwide phenomenon, and it is expected to continue. Monetary inflation means a period of rising prices for goods and services (the value of the dollar falls); deflation is the converse, a period of declining prices. Because the LCC effort is not directed toward predicting the future, but rather toward planning wisely for future situations, the assumed inflation rate does not have to be precise for the LCC results to be useful. The better the estimate, though, the less chance of misleading results.

The inflation rate is usually expressed as the ratio between the prices of two different years. For example, if the price of diesel fuel is 35 cents per gallon in 1977 and 38 cents in 1978, then the inflation ratio is 38/35, or 1.086, which is also stated as 8.6 percent. On the basis of these data, in 1978, the projected, inflated cost of diesel fuel for 1979 could be assumed to be 1.086 times 38 cents, or 41 cents (assuming a constant inflation rate).

Inflation Indices

The U.S. Department of Labor periodically collects price statistics on a number of consumer goods and services and averages these to obtain a consumer price index. Other such indices are the wholesale price index and the gross national product price deflator (a deflator is a ratio used to adjust monetary statistics for the change in value). A multiplicity of indices is necessary because prices do not change uniformly, and each of us uses a different mix of goods and services. Coffee prices may spurt upward while sugar declines. Those who do not use sugar may not perceive the same rate of inflation as those who do use sugar. The particular effect of inflation on a program depends on the selection of goods and services required by that program during its lifetime.

For military LCC purposes, the DOD has published deflators for military pay, military personnel costs other than pay, operations and maintenance, civilian pay, military construction, and so on (see Table 6-1). Each of the services also has provided these data; for example, the USAF in AFR 173-10.[1]

Individual companies often find it useful to have their own pricing index. Such an index combines the inflation trends of the particular mix of labor, materials, capital goods, and other expenses that a company has experienced. The index can be useful in converting historical cost experience into current estimates, as is necessary for all estimates by analogy,

CERs, and industrial engineering methods. Furthermore, it can be used for forecasting future costs by projecting the trend of past experience into the future. Most companies have found that their price experience differs sufficiently from that contained in such public indices as those of the Department of Labor to warrant the preparation and use of their own index on major bids.

Neither the calculation nor the projection of price indices is simple. The selection of costs to include in the index and their weighting requires careful judgment. The projection of the index requires the use of forecasting techniques such as regression analyses, including linear, nonlinear, and multi-variate and time series. Econometric forecasting models can be quite complex.[2]

Inflation Calculations

Inflation indices are used in two ways. First, inflation factors are used to convert historical data into estimates of today's costs. If a tank chassis cost $300,000 in 1974, and the inflation index from 1974 to 1978 was 1.4293, then the estimated price in 1978 is ($300,000) x (1.4293), or $428,790. This figure could serve as a starting point for an estimate by analogy or as one data point for the development of a CER. Second, inflation factors can convert present-day estimates into future-year costs. For example, if the cost of a new tank chassis, somewhat improved from the one discussed above, is estimated at $500,000 in 1978, what will it cost in 1981? The inflation index between 1978 and 1981 is estimated at 1.139,[3] and so ($500,000) x (1.139) is $569,500.

An LCC estimate should be presented either in "current dollars" ("then year dollars") or in constant dollars (usually using the starting year of the program). Either mode of presentation is satisfactory, but the current dollar is preferred. By incorporating inflation, this method allows analysts to track the estimate in current dollars as the program pro-

Table 6-1
DEPARTMENT OF
DEFENSE DEFLATORS

BASE YEAR IS FY 78

	MILPER PAY	MILPER OTHER	MILPER TOTAL	RMC	RETIRED PAY	CIVILIAN PAY
1945	15.7323	27.3426	17.3039	19.1396	13.0193	14.5980
1946	16.0361	28.1558	18.0017	19.1692	15.2559	15.4567
1947	20.0649	29.3917	21.5540	24.8082	19.9571	15.8618
1948	20.0378	31.2902	21.8164	24.5896	21.1611	17.2912
1949	19.9275	31.6961	21.2931	24.6638	21.2730	18.6573
1950	22.6776	33.1143	23.8229	27.9967	20.3945	19.5160
1951	23.3534	32.7647	24.3011	29.1377	32.3951	19.3599
1952	23.7998	35.7024	25.2936	29.6573	32.2186	20.0479
1953	25.4085	35.9946	26.5479	32.2444	32.7344	21.3835
1954	25.2917	35.2139	26.4909	32.3778	30.5521	22.4434
1955	25.8658	36.2880	27.1103	32.4932	32.4170	23.8095
1956	27.1673	37.8209	28.5993	32.8742	34.6390	25.4489
1957	26.6354	39.3548	28.1223	32.9637	35.9830	26.3855
1958	28.0561	43.2031	30.0202	37.1318	36.3054	29.8205
CY58	29.0659	43.5708	30.9670	33.0045	37.6148	31.1685
1959	29.9965	43.9166	31.6935	34.9253	38.8448	31.8111
1960	30.5667	43.3978	32.0528	34.9674	38.5274	32.7479
1961	30.6261	44.7041	32.5470	34.9794	38.4084	35.2459
1962	30.4071	45.1525	32.5339	34.9123	38.4431	35.0265
1963	30.7169	45.1826	32.6557	35.5901	38.1306	37.3927
1964	33.3865	47.0115	35.2521	38.7950	39.6781	39.0520
1965	34.6937	48.6799	36.5506	39.1850	40.3526	41.3349
1966	38.1838	50.8849	40.1570	41.0930	42.1778	42.8181
1967	40.0943	54.4498	42.4937	42.0643	43.7252	44.6915
CY67	40.8988	56.0714	43.5783	43.4374	44.5188	45.3162
1968	42.1136	57.3707	44.8759	44.8453	45.1933	46.3317
1969	45.4845	58.4635	47.8058	47.3956	47.6137	49.0365
1970	52.4671	60.3727	53.8413	54.3426	51.1847	55.1132
1971	56.5861	63.2496	57.4900	58.2103	56.6206	59.6790
1972	66.3284	65.9800	66.2787	67.1631	60.3960	64.4809
1973	73.6736	69.0824	73.3935	74.1329	64.0653	68.0718
1974	79.6090	76.7558	79.2715	79.8960	70.2520	73.9266
1975	84.5098	87.1033	84.8533	85.2842	30.1592	80.0546
1976	88.8399	92.2052	89.2972	34.7714	39.0066	39.9875
TY76	90.0045	94.0574	30.5847	30.8824	90.4577	85.0664
1977	94.1849	95.8825	94.4134	95.3469	94.2103	93.7158
1978	100.0000	100.0000	100.0000	100.0000	100.0000	100.0000

Table 6-1. Department of Defense Deflators (Continued)

04/04/77

	* ~* * * * * * * * * * PURCHASES * * * * * * * * * * *				COMMERCE INDUSTRY	PURCHASE COMPUTER
	O + M	RDT+E	MIL CON	OTHER NON-PAY	PURCHASE	COMPOSITE
1945	24.4158	23.8614	23.5956	24.9040	.4572	23.3390
1946	26.3824	25.7519	22.2545	26.9099	.4572	25.0122
1947	31.3175	30.4960	26.4174	31.9437	.4572	28.6726
1948	35.9558	34.9740	30.3300	36.6747	34.1973	33.6511
1949	38.1450	36.0446	32.1767	38.9078	36.6204	35.7288
1950	37.1061	35.5900	31.3003	37.8480	34.8831	34.7044
1951	40.5516	37.3658	33.1863	41.4644	37.8548	38.1037
1952	39.2431	39.0157	36.1157	40.0277	37.6719	37.8365
1953	39.7773	39.6814	36.3565	40.5727	36.8490	38.4572
1954	39.0002	40.1743	35.4736	39.7800	36.9405	37.5185
1955	41.5743	40.7740	34.8717	42.4056	38.4949	39.1040
1956	43.2742	41.8818	36.4367	44.1395	40.1407	40.3838
1957	46.5763	43.4147	38.7642	47.5082	42.3809	43.3559
1958	47.1111	44.4362	39.2457	48.0531	42.7010	43.9414
CY58	47.4397	44.7594	38.9048	48.4494	42.7924	44.2722
1959	48.2282	45.2357	38.6839	49.1925	42.9753	44.3469
1960	47.8396	45.1792	33.2024	48.7962	43.4782	43.9800
1961	48.8110	46.7145	38.1622	49.7870	43.6611	44.7513
1962	48.2282	47.3701	38.7240	49.1925	44.5297	44.8835
1963	48.3733	48.1611	39.5667	49.3411	45.4441	44.7094
1964	48.5682	48.8624	40.1285	49.5393	45.7184	45.5825
1965	49.1059	49.7585	41.2923	50.0877	46.4042	45.9181
1966	50.7361	51.1100	42.7369	51.7506	47.9129	48.0076
1967	52.5547	52.7518	44.2333	53.0655	49.6044	50.3290
CY67	53.4615	53.5409	45.3170	54.5304	50.4731	49.3615
1968	54.3419	54.6604	46.4008	55.4285	51.3417	52.5618
1969	56.0649	57.2403	49.7416	57.1859	53.3534	53.9363
1970	58.2704	60.4046	53.8702	59.4355	55.7764	56.2563
1971	60.9189	63.4976	58.7723	62.1370	58.6110	59.0686
1972	63.2548	66.4215	62.5925	64.5196	61.0798	61.4844
1973	65.8794	63.3264	66.4107	67.1966	63.7314	63.6979
1974	69.7707	74.8400	75.5754	71.6273	69.9034	69.9894
1975	80.2744	83.0201	89.8591	81.8795	81.4244	81.1477
1976	86.2900	88.5215	91.2968	88.0154	87.5507	87.1999
TY76	89.1470	91.0607	92.1285	90.9295	90.1109	89.6228
1977	93.3655	94.3596	94.3396	94.3377	93.9525	93.7425
1978	100.0000	100.0000	100.0000	100.0000	100.0000	100.0000

S: U.S., Office of the Assistant Secretary of Defense (Program/Budget) gresses; it also enables budget planners to use the data more directly. In comparison, constant-dollar presentation keeps the future costs looking reasonable and makes the total LCC estimate look less formidable. Both modes are workable, and neither changes the dialectic planning process.

Discounting

After the effect of inflation has been accounted for, there still remains another difference between future dollars and current dollars. Would you rather have a dollar today, or the firm promise of a dollar a year from now? Most bankers will offer the firm promise of a dollar a year from now for the payment of 94 cents; in other words, if you give them 94 cents today, they will promise to pay back $1.00 in a year. This is an interest rate of about 6.38 percent, and represents the *time value* of money.

There may be other, more lucrative ways to invest money than in a bank; these better opportunities for investment should be the criterion by which the time value of money is judged. Technically, this is called the opportunity cost of money. If the money is spent now, what opportunities must be foregone? These potential investment opportunities could yield a much higher return than a typical bank investment; clearly, the purpose of any enterprise is to conduct operations that will be more profitable than an interest-bearing bank account. Therefore, the time value of money for most enterprises is more than the bank interest rate or the bond interest rate. The time value of money depends on the type of enterprise and the potential return on its invested capital.

The potential return of government investments is particularly difficult to assess. Government activities often produce only intangible benefits; even the measurable benefits are difficult to express in dollars. Government activities are investments, nevertheless, and benefits are expected to exceed the cost, or there would be no point in making the investment. A rate of return should then be evaluated and serve as the basis of a discount rate.

The comptroller general of the United States reported to the Joint Economic Committee of the Congress in 1968 that the few federal agencies that used discounting techniques used widely varying methods and discount rates.[4] In 1969, the Joint Economic Committee continued that study and suggested that a 9 percent discount rate was conservative for governmental expenditures.[5] The committee noted that if the money were not spent by the government, it would be available for private spending; private enterprise usually returns more than 9 percent, so governmental projects should show at least a 9 percent return or the money should be left for private use.

Present DOD practice is to use a 10 percent discount rate. Consequently, the DOD considers that the expenditure of $1,000 today is equivalent to a plan to spend $1,100 next year, $1,210 in two years, or $1,331 in three years, as it would have the use of the money during the intervening time. This, of course, assumes that prices remain stable in the interim, or that inflationary effects are eliminated. The discounting factors provided in Table 6-2 are used to calculate the present value of future obligations. Computer programs for LCC models (see Chapter 9) often have discount rates built into them. The desired discount rate can be selected, and the input data values will be appropriately adjusted.

Discount Calculations

Note that the effect of discounting on LCC estimates is to make projects that can defer spending more attractive than projects that require money sooner. For example, Table 6-3 compares two programs that do the same task. Note that both programs have the same total expenditure, but program B is able to defer major expenses to a later date and so is less expensive as of 1978.

Table 6-2

DISCOUNT FACTORS

Year	6%	8%	10%	12%	14%
1	.9434	.9259	.9091	.8929	.8772
2	.8900	.8573	.8264	.7972	.7695
3	.8396	.7938	.7513	.7118	.6750
4	.7921	.7350	.6830	.6355	.5921
5	.7473	.6806	.6209	.5674	.5194
6	.7050	.6302	.5645	.5066	.4556
7	.6651	.5835	.5132	.4523	.3996
8	.6274	.5403	.4665	.4039	.3506
9	.5919	.5002	.4241	.3606	.3075
10	.5584	.4632	.3855	.3220	.2697
11	.5268	.4289	.3505	.2875	.2366
12	.4970	.3971	.3186	.2567	.2076
13	.4688	.3677	.2897	.2292	.1821
14	.4423	.3405	.2633	.2046	.1597
15	.4173	.3152	.2394	.1827	.1401
16	.3936	.2919	.2176	.1631	.1229
17	.3714	.2703	.1978	.1456	.1078
18	.3503	.2502	.1799	.1300	.0946
19	.3305	.2317	.1635	.1161	.0829
20	.3118	.2145	.1486	.1037	.0728
21	.2942	.1987	.1351	.0926	.0638
22	.2775	.1839	.1228	.0826	.0560
23	.2618	.1703	.1117	.0738	.0491
24	.2470	.1577	.1015	.0659	.0431
25	.2330	.1460	.0923	.0588	.0378
26	.2198	.1352	.0839	.0525	.0331
27	.2074	.1252	.0763	.0469	.0291
28	.1956	.1159	.0693	.0419	.0255
29	.1846	.1073	.0630	.0374	.0224
30	.1741	.0994	.0573	.0334	.0196

Table 6-3

PROGRAMS WITH EQUAL COSTS BEFORE DISCOUNTING

Year	1978	1979	1980	1981	1982	1983	1984	Total
Program A								
Cost	15	15	175	100	50	50	50	455
Discounted	15	14	145	75	34	31	28	342
Program B								
Cost	10	20	100	125	100	50	50	455
Discounted	10	18	83	94	68	31	28	332
Discount Rate	–	1.1	1.21	1.33	1.46	1.61	1.77	

This result may prove troublesome to devotees of LCC, in that the LCC method often encourages program managers to spend money on R&D and early production so as to save money later during O&S. When early spending on R&D can decrease total LCC, even with discounting, the impact of the change on decision makers is dramatically increased. The example of Table 6-4 shows that program A, by early investment, was able to cut future costs, and the total *discounted* LCC is lower than that of program B. If the example were extended over a number of years (as would be true for most real life programs), the results would be even more striking.

The arguments over the total costs of the nuclear breeder reactor versus those of conventional reactors are an example of the effect of the discount rate, made more impressive by the long life of reactors. Nuclear breeder reactors have higher investment costs but lower fuel costs than conventional reactors, and both have assumed lifetimes of fifty years. If discount rates of 4 or 5 percent are used, the breeder reactor's lower fuel costs are significant; if a discount rate of 10 percent is used, the conventional reactor has a lower LCC.

The discounting technique is used for the analysis of governmental investments in lieu of the *present value* approach to capital investment financial analysis used in private enterprise. Government programs usually do not have the stream of earnings assumed in capital investment financial analysis; therefore, the present value method has been modified into the discounting method shown above. Other capital investment financial analysis methods such as *return on investment* and *payout period* are more difficult to adapt to the government situation and are not recommended.[6]

Zero Discount

Some LCC analyses do not use discounting, either for reasons of simplicity, or from a lack of understanding. The result is a zero (percent) discount rate, which has important

Table 6-4

INITIAL INVESTMENT SAVES OUT-YEAR COSTS

Year	1978	1979	1980	1981	1982	1983	1984	Total
Program A								
Cost	15	15	175	100	40	40	40	425
Discounted	15	14	145	75	27	25	23	324
Program B								
Cost	10	20	100	125	100	50	50	455
Discounted	10	18	83	94	68	31	28	332
Discount Rate	–	1.1	1.21	1.33	1.46	1.61	1.77	

implications. It assumes (1) that there are no opportunities available to invest the money at any gain, (2) that the interest rate is zero, and (3) that if there is inflation, the interest rate is negative. In this situation, it is desirable to spend money in the early stages of the program, stockpiling inventory and spares and producing at the optimum rate. Rolf Clark defends this view.[7] The informed customer, however, will insist that LCC analyses use an agreed-upon discount rate in order to prevent such distortion.

Implied Discount Rates

The preceding discussion may suggest that the discount rate can be derived as a precise mathematical formulation. Not so. The Congress, for example, behaves as if the discount rate were very high but does not explicitly state this position. When given the choice between spending one dollar today or spending much more in the future, it often defers the spending. This implies that members of Congress have a high internal discount rate; some have estimated this rate, as judged by their behavior, at 50 percent. This may not be excessive; congressional constituents would most likely favor such a discount rate so as to defer taxes, perhaps not realizing that a day of reckoning inevitably comes.

Combined Inflation and Discount Calculations

The effect of inflation and discounting can be combined in a single equation to provide an adjustment factor for each year's costs,

$$\text{Adjustment factor} = \left(\frac{1 + \text{IR}}{1 + \text{DR}}\right)^n$$

where

IR = The average inflation rate per year

DR = The average discount rate per year

n = The number of years

Note that if the average inflation rate equals the average discount rate, the adjustment factor is unity; this implies an effective interest rate of zero. The equation is based on the expenditure of the funds at the end of *n* years. If, as is usually the case, the funds are expended *during* the *n*th year, the calculation should be for the *n* - ½ year. Such refinements, though academically correct, exceed the accuracy of the input data and the assumptions and add only elegance.

Economic Theory

The mechanics of discounting are based on the economic theory of the time value of money. This theory involves a number of concepts, such as the social opportunity cost of capital, the rate-of-time concept, risk, and inflation. Robert Shishko discusses these in some detail in a Rand Corporation study of the defense procurement situation.[8] He concludes that (1) if any discount rate should be used for governmental decisions, 10 percent is a reasonable value; (2) implicit in the decision to use discounting is an assumption about the probable state of the world at the time when the system may be used; (3) the method, as well as the rate, of discounting selected may determine the choice between alternative programs; and (4) risk considerations and the assumed inflation rate should influence the choice of a discount rate. The last point is particularly important because discounting is often used unintentionally to combine the effects of risk and inflation, as well as the time value of money.

Summary

1. Indices of past inflation can correct past cost data and provide current prices for estimating purposes. Indices of predicted inflation can also project present-day estimates into future costs.

2. LCC estimates present data either in constant dollars or in current dollars. Constant dollars look smaller and may be easier to reprogram. Current (then-year) dollars correlate with contract performance and work well for budget planning.

3. Discounting compensates for the time value of money. The U.S. DOD uses a 10 percent discount rate as a standard.

4. Although discounting provides a valuable insight into the relative present value of different cash flows, academicians, legislators, and even some LCC analysts do not agree on discounting theory or practice.

Notes

1. U.S. Air Force, *USAF Cost and Planning Factors,* AFR 173-10, vols. 1, 2 (Washington, D.C.: Department of the Air Force, 1977); U.S. Navy, *Navy Program Factors Manual,* OPNAV 90P-02, vols. 1, 2 (Philadelphia: Naval Publications and Forms Center, 1977); U.S. Army, Comptroller of the Army, Directorate of Cost Analysis, *Army Force Planning Cost Handbook* (Washington, D.C.: Department of the Army, 1977).

2. Thomas P. Lennerty, *An Investigation of the Forecasting of Aeronautical Price Indices* (Wright-Patterson Air Force Base, Ohio: Air Force Institute of Technology, 1976), various forecasting techniques; George E. P. Box and Gwilyn M. Jenkins, *Time Series Analysis: Forecasting and Control* (San Francisco: Holden-Day, 1970).

3. An estimated annual inflation rate of 1.044.

4. U.S. Congress, Joint Economic Committee, Subcommittee on Economy in Government, *Survey of Use by Federal Agencies of the Discounting Technique in Evaluating Future Programs,* 90th Cong., 2d sess., 1968.

5. U.S. Congress, Joint Economic Committee, *The Analysis and Evaluation of Public Expenditures,* 91st Cong., 1st sess., 1969, p. 490.

6. For a discussion of private industry capital investment, see Charles W. Haley and Lawrence D. Schall, *The Theory of Financial Decisions* (New York: McGraw-Hill, 1973).

7. Rolf H. Clark, "Should Defense Managers Discount Future Costs?" *Defense Management Journal,* March 1978, pp. 12-14.

8. Robert Shishko, *Choosing the Discount Rate for Defense Decision Making* (Santa Monica, Calif.: Rand Corp. 1976).

7
Contractual Arrangements

How can competitive contracts be won with minimum risk and an acceptable profit potential? How can contracts be let with minimum risk and an acceptable potential LCC, within budget constraints?

The purpose of this book is to present a better method of government procurement than the current methods in use. This chapter will discuss contractual arrangements for LCC that will assure a favorable program for all parties concerned. For the buyer, the risk of price increases, schedule slips, and inferior performance are feared; for the seller, a loss of money or reputation is to be avoided. Both signatories to a procurement contract prefer to minimize risks; the buyer also wants an acceptable price (one that falls within budgetary constraints) and an acceptable LCC; the seller seeks an acceptable profit (return on investment). An acceptable profit and an acceptable price and LCC are not incompatible goals; a degree of accord is achieved in most sales transactions because neither party needs to maximize these goals. On the other hand, the levels of risk assumed by the two parties are complementary; the less risk taken by one party, the more risk to be assumed by the other. The analysis of contractual arrangements is based on the propensity of each party to

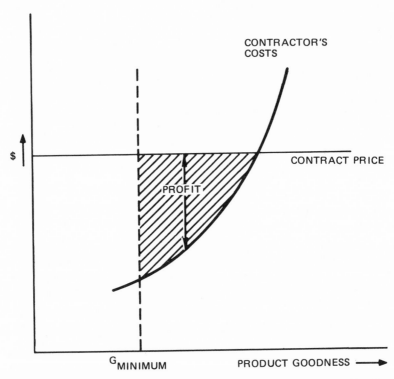

Figure 7-1. Minimizing Product Goodness Maximizes Profit

minimize its risk, for almost all government contracts for the development of large systems have a significant degree of risk.

In the past, the government assumed the major portion of the risk for large procurements. The notorious case was the "cost plus" contract, wherein the contractor was reimbursed for all costs, plus a fixed percentage of those costs as a fee (few such contracts were actually let). Many contracts have been let on a fixed-price basis. The problem with such contracts is illustrated in Figure 7-1, which shows that the contractor's costs increase and the profits decrease as the system's performance capabilities are improved, or with other good innovations. Even in a cost-type, fixed-fee contract, the *percentage* profit decreases as the costs rise. The contractor

Table 7-1. Incentive Payment Schedule

Performance	Incentive Fee
All 5 flights successful	$100,000
4 of 5 flights successful	$50,000
3 of 5 flights successful	None
Less than 3 flights successful	Deficiency must be corrected
- - - - - - - - - - - - - - -	- - - - - - - - - - - -
All contractual deliveries on or before schedule	$10,000
All contractual hardware deliveries on or before schedule	$5,000

is therefore motivated to produce the minimum performance that will be accepted, i.e., that meet the contract requirements. Worse yet, the contractor may believe that poor reliability or supportability (logistics resources requirements) might result in lucrative follow-on contracts for spares, other support, and changes. Incentive-fee contracts have been devised to motivate the contractor to improve the products delivered.

Incentive Fees and Penalties

Incentive fees are extra payments to the contractor for an improved product; penalties are a reduction in the price paid for failure to meet the nominal requirements. These payments or reductions are based on system performance, tests, production costs (design to cost), delivery schedule, or estimated logistic support cost. A contractual arrangement of

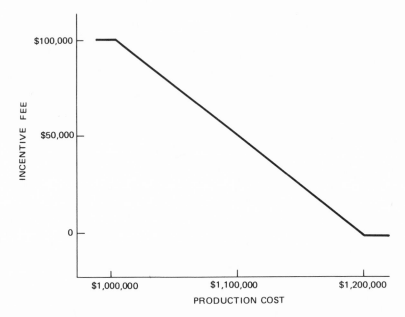

Figure 7-2. DTC Incentive Fee Has a Limited Range

this kind is intended to insure that the seller's management pay attention to specified parameters by assuming some of the risk of not meeting them. The payment schedule might be in the form of a table, such as Table 7-1, or of a graph, such as Figure 7-2.

Incentive fee arrangements have been used with success for a number of years. The arrangement should be made as early as possible in the program; both buyer and seller should understand the purpose and the mechanics of the incentive fee. The purpose is to motivate the contractor, and a clear understanding of the improvements desired and the rewards and punishments possible is essential for such motivation.

The incentive payment should be large enough to motivate the contractor. The rate of increase of the payment should be greater than the cost of improving the product. This possibility is shown in Figure 7-3. Note that *B*, the profit to be made with the incentive payment, must be larger than *A*, the profit that can be made without the payment, for it to

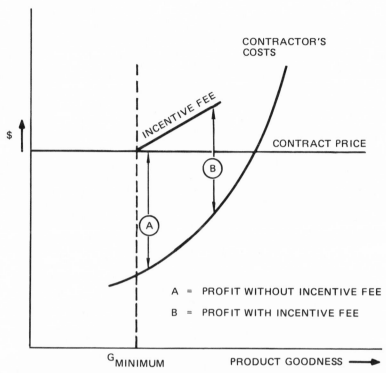

Figure 7-3. Incentive Fee Slope Determines Contractor's Profit Change

motivate the contractor in the desired direction. If *A* and *B* are the same, all other things being equal, the contractor is indifferent to the incentive payment possibility. In this case, the payment merely eliminates the penalty against the contractor for making too good a product. Only if the incentive is greater than the cost of an improved product will the contractor perceive that adequate attention to the specified parameters will decrease risk.[1]

Incentive fees often have associated administrative problems. Careful attention to precise contractual language, covering most eventualities, is recommended. If the incentive is based on test results, as in Table 7-1, prior agreement on the success criteria is vital. Many hours have been spent arguing over whether a "near miss" of a simulated target should be scored as a hit of an actual target. Furthermore, if not all the contemplated number of tests are completed, decision criteria for the incentives with this new schedule should be provided.

Incentive fees can also create design and planning problems. When incentive fees accomplish their purpose, the contractor devotes maximum attention to the specified parameters, often to the neglect of other desirable features that may be difficult to specify and control but are usually understood by both parties. These features may include various kinds of documentation, the provision of convenience and safety features, assistance with relations with other customer agencies, and so on. When the customer provides strong financial incentives for a contractor, no one should be surprised that the contractor concentrates on only those incentive features. A recent attempt to cope with this problem is the award fee contract.

Award Fee

The award fee is based on the customer program manager's judgment of the performance of the contractor. The customer provides a list of the criteria by which the contractor's performance will be judged, along with a schedule noting the points at which such judgments will be made. The list might include such items as the contractor's performance in minimizing logistic costs or the contractor's management of logistic support requirements. The schedule might include a design review, a program review, or a system acquisition review council. At the conclusion of each review, the customer program manager and his staff evaluate the performance of the contractor for the period on a zero to 100 percent basis. The contractor receives that proportion of the potential fee. If the potential fee for data submittals is $5,000 and if the contractor is judged to have achieved 80 percent of the possible performance, then a $4,000 fee is awarded.

It is of course obvious that extraneous factors may influence the judgment of the program manager. Moreover, it is difficult for the program manager and his staff to reach completely impartial and objective conclusions about the performance of the contractor. Nevertheless, the award fee does lessen some of the problems of the incentive fee and, given capable program managers for both parties, is a positive step forward.

Design to Cost

As discussed earlier, the phrase *design to cost* has generally been used to mean *design to production cost*, rather than *design to life cycle cost*, despite the stated desire of DOD management for the latter. Many current DOD requests for proposal for development contracts require an estimate of the unit production cost and a commitment to provide the product at that production cost. A variant of this approach requires that the contractor continuously revise his design to the unit production cost (DTUPC) goal and that at some point that goal will be fixed for use in the production contract. This form is usually used in a development phase involving more than one contractor.

The DTUPC approach is intended to motivate the management and the design, production, and other personnel to decrease production costs. They are given a specific cost goal. Production cost becomes a design parameter, like performance parameters. Often the goal is expressed as the unit repetitive production cost, deleting the nonrecurring start-up costs and the tooling and test equipment costs, on the grounds that such costs are not usually under the control of the designers. The unit repetitive cost includes the fabrication labor hours and the purchased material. The designer can calculate these and understand their sensitivty to design characteristics.

An incentive fee can be made proportional to performance

against the DTUPC goal, as shown in Figure 7-2. Note that the fee is proportional to deviation from the DTUPC goal for a relatively small range; outside of that range, the fee is fixed. This is commonly done to control the risk to the contractor and to assure that the profit will not rise above legal limits. As with other incentive arrangements, the DTUPC formula may cause the contractor to sacrifice other desirable attributes, such as LCC, to achieve the maximum DTUPC incentive. The buyer must carefully and constantly guard against such degradation of desirable attributes. Even better, awards for all of the desirable attributes would motivate the contractor in the buyer's interests. Methods of conducting DTUPC programs are discussed in Chapter 9.

Reliability Improvement Warranty (RIW)

The reliability improvement warranty (also known as a failure-free warranty) is a fixed-price contractual incentive for operational reliability and maintainability improvement.[2] The contract requires the repair of failures of the equipment during use for a specified period of time. The equipment is returned to the contractor's facility for repair and return, perhaps within a fixed period of time. Inherent in this fixed-price arrangement is the incentive for the contractor to enhance the reliability and maintainability of the product so as to minimize his repair costs. To facilitate this, the contract usually allows the contractor to institute product changes at no cost to the buyer. If the contractor determines that the cost to him of a change will be more than offset by the savings in repair costs, he is motivated to propose such a change. The customer should facilitate such changes, as they enhance the product at no cost. The contract should delineate whether these reliability improvements can be applied only to the returned failed units or must be incorporated in all units (either in the field or by recall). RIW contracts usually run for up to five years; they should last at least three years to give the contractor a significant incentive for improvement changes. The orderly phase-in of government maintenance at the end of the RIW period continues the savings realized by the RIW.

Usually RIW contracts also provide a reliability or mean time between failures (MTBF) guarantee. This requires that during the guarantee period, the MTBF of the product be measured by dividing the total accumulated operating time by the number of failures during that time. If the measured MTBF is less than the guaranteed MTBF, the contractor is required to correct the deficiency at his own expense.

The contract should mention methods of accounting for equipment that does not evidence failure when returned to the contractor's facility. RIW is a significant step beyond a prepaid maintenance contract. It motivates the contractor to improve the initial design for reliability and maintainability. Second, it encourages the contractor to propose engineering changes after the product is in the field so as to improve reliability and maintainability further and to reduce the risk that repair costs, or the MTBF correction costs, will cause cost overruns. Third, it provides a reduced customer investment in handbooks, spares, test equipment, and maintenance training until these requirements have stabilized. Next, it provides an early, explicit value for maintenance costs for planning purposes. Finally, RIW permits a temporary relaxation in configuration control so that competition is possible for a product defined on a form, fit, and function basis.

The RIW situation is open to gaming as the contractor attempts to maximize profit rather than furnish the best product for the user. In writing an RIW contract clause, the buyer should assure himself that the contractor will try to improve the product's reliability at a price that lowers the LCC. The RIW analysis to be done by the contractor and the buyer are the same. Gates et al. have formulated an excellent quantitative method for alternative ways of implementing an RIW clause, but it is dependent on the difficult forecast of the reliability of equipment, and the cost of changing that reliability.[3] Methods for approaching this are discussed in Chapter 9. The results will be specific for an individual equipment, not for all equipments generally. The contract should include an option plan to allow the buyer to extend the RIW period. If the buyer elects not to extend the period, the contractor should be reimbursed for the cost of reliability improvements made in the expectation that the RIW period would be extended.

Weimer has written a retrospective analysis of a number of RIW contracts.[4] He shows that most RIW contracts have not been successful in motivating contractors to increase effort on design, testing, and quality control but rather have encouraged them to pay more attention to project and financial management. Again, this situation demonstrates the importance of designing the RIW clause properly. The incentive fee payoff must be sufficiently rewarding, as shown in Figure 7-3, to express the buyer's desires clearly. Moreover, to assure a maximum favorable LCC effect, the contractor must be influenced to enhance customer organic maintainability as well as to ease the burden of contractor maintenance.

The reliability demonstration warranty is another form of reliability incentive, without the maintenance requirement. Unfortunately, such a demonstration warranty occurs so late that it does not seem to influence the design process even as much as the RIW.

The costs of RIW and similar contractual clauses can be charged either to procurement funds or to operating and support funds; some even suggest that the money is really being spent for continued development. Because the clause is part of the procurement contract, the most expeditious course is to use procurement funds.

Logistic Support Cost Warranty

The RIW covers maintenance costs, which are only a part

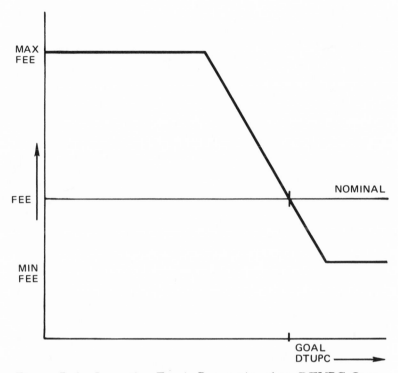

Figure 7-4. Incentive Fee is Proportional to DTUPC Over
A Limited Range

of the logistic support costs. In an effort to motivate contractors to become concerned about other support costs,
various forms of logistic support cost warranties have been
tried by the military services. The basic problem with these
warranties is that although the logistic characteristics are
determined during the design contract, the logistic costs will
not be known until the production contract has been completed and the product is operational in the field. Such a
delay is incompatible with a meaningful system of rewards
and penalties.

A solution has been to use a simulation of the logistic situation to evaluate the logistic support cost of the product. The
contract specifies a target logistic support cost (TLSC), with
a schedule of fees, like that of Figure 7-4, which was used for

DTUPC. The logistic support cost model is used to determine, at the end of the development contract, the logistic support cost of the product. This logistic support cost model would have equations for those costs over which the contractor has substantial control, such as provisioning, maintenance, data, training, support equipment, and fuel consumption. The air force Logistic Support Cost model is typical; the RCA PRICE life cycle cost model can also be used with some additional equations. The design data developed by the contractor provide the inputs to the model. The contractor therefore has available during development phase a reference to the prospective logistic costs and can take remedial action as necessary (while keeping within the restraints of the performance requirements, schedule, and production costs). Even if some of the constants in the real world change, such as personnel turnover rate, there is no change in the equations of the simulation or in the contractual relationship.

An early determination of logistic costs may pose problems for both buyer and seller. An example of the problems that a contractor may face in satisfying a logistic support clause occurs in the selection of a product failure analysis system. If contractor personnel are to maintain the equipment (augmented support or RIW), then the equipment can be designed so that failure analysis using complex test equipment will take place at a central, depotlike facility. The test set will be operated by skilled technicians on permanent assignment to the task. If, on the other hand, military personnel are to maintain the equipment in the field, then the equipment must be designed so that simplified, rugged test sets can be used by less-trained personnel on relatively short tours of duty. The choice of a failure analysis system will also influence the design and size of the replaceable modules; the more elaborate test methods can isolate faults to small modules, but the simpler tests can only isolate problems to larger areas. During the development phase, the buyer may be unable to specify whether the contractor or the user will be

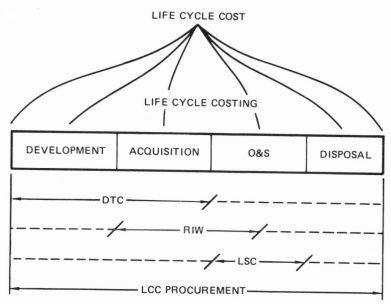

Figure 7–5. Coverage of Contractual Method

responsible for maintenance. A nonbinding statement of intent should be made at that time to guide design.

Particular attention should be given to the provisioning equations in the simulation. The usual methods of determining requirements for spares and repair parts are less than rational; they depend on the funding available, individual proclivities, and bargaining abilities. The simulation equations tend to reflect what provisioning should cost rather than forecast the expected result. This emphasizes one benefit of RIW—the user can postpone the provisioning decisions until after the contractor has accumulated experience on repair requirements.

Life Cycle Cost Procurement

As shown in Figure 7-5, each of the contractual methods discussed above provides control over a portion of life cycle costs. These are all positive steps beyond procurement on the basis of first cost alone. The goal is to minimize the total costs to the user, and achievement of that goal requires an additional step beyond the use of these contractual methods. That step is LCC procurement.

In LCC procurement, proposals for the initial competition for a development contract must include an estimate of LCC. These LCC estimates must be made in accordance with a set of ground rules and assumptions, like those shown in Table 7-2, which are supplied by the procurement agency in the request for proposal. The request should provide an accounting model so that each of the proposals submitted covers the same costs and so that the basis of the estimates can be seen. The agency should also define the scope of LCC and furnish operational cost data, along with an operational and support scenario in sufficient detail to enable contractors to prepare plans required for O&S estimating. Contractors should be obliged to make a commitment as to the validity of their LCC estimate.

Invariably, the request for proposal will lack some information that contractors need. Some mechanism should be provided to encourage competitors to ask questions and to provide all of them with all of the answers.

In preparing a competitive request for proposal, the amount of detailed directions and information furnished the bidders represents a balance of opposing motivations. On the one hand, the more instructions and directions given, the easier it will be to compare the resultant LCC estimates and to evaluate the bids. On the other hand, with relatively little direction, the bidders will exercise ingenuity and creativity in their LCC estimates; truly innovative notions may be developed that can assist the program considerably. In general, the period of competition is not the best time to elicit such inventive thinking; it is always difficult to select the best source. The additional objective of obtaining more LCC ideas may overload the process.

The selection criteria for the award of contract should be

Table 7-2
GROUND RULES AND ASSUMPTIONS FOR LIFE
CYCLE COST ESTIMATE

1. Government and contractor costs included.

2. All estimates in 1978 dollars. DOD inflation factors used to revise earlier data.

3. Ten-year system lifetime from initial operational capability.

4. No combat operations. No combat losses or replacements.

5. Minimum testing during deployment; no periodic depot surveillance tests.

6. Salvage price equals disposal cost; therefore, neither included.

7. Cost will be displayed in accordance with Department of the Army Pamphlet 11-5.

8. LCC estimate must correlate with contract estimate; all deviations must be explained.

9. The derivation of all data must be comprehensively explained and illustrated by supporting displays.

10. Procurement costs of inventory equipment may be obtained from Army Supply Bulletin.

11. All land is furnished at no cost; no real property taxes.

12. Meteorological services furnished at no cost.

13. All encryption and decryption equipment is government furnished and a sunk cost.

14. The Air Force Logistic Command logistic support cost model is to be used where applicable.

part of the request; the realism and value of the LCC estimate should certainly be part of those criteria. Astute contractors will often include cost categories unfamiliar to less experienced competitors. The decision method should reward, not penalize, such insights. The contract when awarded should include RIW, DTUPC, TLSC, and LCC clauses.

The contract must mandate LCC activity and require the contractor to make periodic reports to the buyer. These reports should explain the impact of all program changes on the LCC estimate. Later changes in LCC estimates can show a good deal about the realism of the initial estimates (more on this in Chapter 10).

The overall strategy provides progressively tightened controls and limits on LCC. In the initial concept, LCC can be estimated with considerable latitude. As development continues, better estimates can be made and tighter controls imposed. This narrowing of the allowable range of costs applies both to the relationship between the user and the developing agency and between the developing agency and the contractors.

Measurement Criteria

Any contract that provides an LCC, RIW, or logistic support cost incentive must supply clear rules for measuring such costs, definitions of the performance expected, and a method of handling contingencies. For example, if a product is supposed to undergo thirty days of testing and weather terminates the operation after twenty-five days, with no possibility of resumption, is the cost to be used the twenty-five-day cost, or the extrapolation of that cost to thirty days? If the desired personnel or test facilities are not available or if provisioning arrangements are changed, how are the costs to be adjusted? Such measurements will be made some time after the contract has been negotiated, and conditions invariably change. Both parties to the contract will try to maximize their positions, and means for adjudicating differences on the spot, as well as in more formal proceedings, must be available. The significant point is that the decision should be made on the basis of the characteristics of the product, not on the basis of the artifacts of the experimental situation.

A typical reliability and maintainability measurement program might use the following ground rules, subject to negotiation:

1. Only "critical" and "major" failures are counted in reliability scoring. "Critical" failures would prevent the system from completing its mission. "Major" failures would prevent the system from tactically performing to specified standards. "Minor" failures may reduce system performance but still permit the system to perform tactically.

2. When a design change has corrected a cause of failure and the change has been verified as effective, the failure shall not be scored.

3. Computer program inadequacies or errors that result in safety hazard or hardware damage are scored.

4. Automatic shutdowns that are manually recycled back up within 5 seconds without corrective maintenance are not scored.

5. A repeat of a scored malfunction without intervening maintenance and checkout shall not be scored. Only the first failure is scored.

6. After repair, recurring failures are counted each time they occur, even if corrective design action has been implemented (a point of contention).

7. Intermittent failures that cannot be repeated are not scored (a point of contention).

8. Secondary failures are considered part of the primary failure; only the primary failure is scored.

9. Any performance failures caused by design rather than by hardware failures are not scored as reliability failures.

10. Failures caused by test equipment or facility failure

are excluded.

11. Failures caused by subjecting the system to environments or test conditions beyond specification requirements are excluded.

12. Failures induced by operator or maintenance personnel error or by incorrect maintenance procedures are excluded.

13. Failures resulting from nonperformance of scheduled maintenance actions are excluded.

Lessons Learned and Problems

The above contractual clauses and methods have been in use in various forms for almost ten years. A number of valuable lessons have been learned and problems discovered:

Do it early. One universal lesson is early inclusion of LCC in the contractual process. No matter how early in the development program LCC has been considered, it seems to be too late. Of course, many will complain that not enough is known about the product during the early phases to forecast production costs, let alone operational costs. Not so. Planning for production and operational costs should begin simultaneously with the conception of the product. At that stage, such planning can have an impact on design. Both the contractor and the customer must come to understand that the predesign period offers the best opportunities to reduce financial risk.

Communicate. The second lesson is to make sure that everybody understands what is wanted and what is intended in the contractual language. Many contractors find late in the procurement process that the procuring agency really intends to enforce the incentive provisions. By then, it may be too late to improve the product without adding prohibitively large costs. The contractor tries to retreat with excuses; the buyer tries to enforce with litigation. No one benefits; everyone loses.

Before the submission of proposals, the buyer should provide a complete explanation of the *intent* of the incentive clauses. The contractor should make sure that all involved personnel are familiar with these ideas. After the contract award, another buyer-contractor meeting should discuss the incentives. The buyer should emphasize the intent of the government to enforce the contract completely. According to Weimer's survey,[5] most military contractors are unconvinced of the government's commitment to LCC and its contractual ramifications and question whether such contract terms are legally enforceable.[6] If properly executed, these cost-incentive contracts are allowed by the Armed Services Procurement Regulations (ASPR) and are legally enforceable. For example, a common contract clause permits a downward price adjustment if the equipment fails to meet the requirements. The purpose of such a penalty, however, must be to compensate the government for harm, not to punish the contractor. In fact, such downward price adjustments seldom compensate the government for more than a small proportion of the increased O&S costs.

The contractual obligation incurred by the proposal estimates should be clearly defined. The best way of doing this is to make the proposal a part of the contract by reference. The contractual agreement should include: (a) definitions of all terms used if they differ from those in a standard dictionary; (b) a statement of the responsibilities of both the contractor and the buyer; and (c) a provision for program changes in test methods, in production quantity, rate, or schedule, and in the locations of users.

Use no-cost changes. The contractor's use of no-cost-to-the-government changes under RIW should be encouraged. As the contractor makes such changes, both parties benefit. The buyer should retain control of such changes so that product uniformity in the field can be maintained.

Plan LCC models carefully. The LCC model should be comprehensive but simple enough for trade studies. A possible solution to this apparent contradiction is to use one model for accounting purposes and a second, compatible model for trade study purposes. See Chapters 8 and 9 for further discussions of models.

Allow flexibility. The contractor must be allowed, and must exercise, the freedom to select the lowest-cost method for design. This freedom is most clearly expressed in the contract specification. This specification should state the results required but not the methods by which to achieve them. A functional specification of performance is ideal, particularly if the specifications are for the top level of the system or equipment being procured.

Creativity flourishes where the mind is free of preconceptions. If a new kind of shoe is desired, describe the task as one of designing a new "foot covering," not a new "shoe." The language used in specifications should also stimulate and free the contractor and the buyer to innovate in the interest of lower cost.

Federal or military specifications and standards can seriously impede the quest for lower costs. Program offices must be free to change, tailor, or eliminate specifications and standards. Because of ingrained habit, many designers will not believe that they have this freedom, even when assured that they do. They should be encouraged, and time should be provided for at least a selective review of potential cost-saving areas.

Avoid tight schedules. A schedule that does not allow for problems forces management to conceal problems from itself. These fester and later cause cost overruns. Expect problems in the schedule, and provide means to redeploy resources to solve the difficulties.

Accelerated schedules, such as development concurrent with production, or production telescoped with deployment, imply a cost risk that should be explicitly recognized and evaluated. Failure to do so invites later unpleasant surprises.

Economic Analysis of Risk

As discussed earlier, the various contractual devices are means for achieving an optimal risk sharing between the government and the contractor. The behavior of the contractor under these imposed risk conditions is complex and may require sophisticated economic analysis. The buyer should analyze the expected behavior of the contractor under the provisions of the contract to assure that he will be satisfied if the contractor behaves rationally. For example, consider a contractor with an R&D contract that requires that he assume 60 percent of all costs above the target. The contractor may elect to exceed the target in order to obtain expertise useful on other programs; the government's 40 percent share of this incremental cost makes it worthwhile to the contractor, even though the profit on the present contract may be low or negative.

More elaborate economic analysis may be required to ascertain whether the contract will, in fact, drive the contractor toward cost minimization for the buyer. Furthermore, such an analysis will provide an optimum behavior recommendation for the contractor. Michael Cummins's analysis of this problem[7] can, with some additional work, be applied to the practical problems of contractual negotiation and implementation.

Summary

1. There are a series of graduated steps for the contractual control of LCC. Performance incentives, award fees, design to cost, reliability improvement warranty, logistic support cost warranty, and LCC procurement provide progressive means of exercising control over the contractor during the procurement cycle.

2. Competition is the most important factor in making LCC contract requirements work easily.

3. To avoid future problems, be sure that contracts are clear, explicit, and understood by both parties.

4. LCC control should start early in the procurement process, require careful planning, allow contractor flexibility, and consider the schedule constraints.

5. If buyers and sellers quantitatively analyze contractual clauses for risk, it will help them determine their best strategy.

Notes

1. Contractors have usually been successful with performance and schedule incentives and unsuccessful with cost incentives. This may reflect the relative expertise of buyer and seller in these areas.

2. Harold S. Balaban and Martin A. Meth, "Contractor Risk Associated with Reliability Improvement Warranty," *Proceedings of the 1978 Annual Reliability and Maintainability Symposium* (New York: Institute of Electrical and Electronic Engineers, 1978); Oscar Markowitz, *Proceedings of the Failure Free Warranty Seminar* (Philadelphia: Aviation Supply Office, 1973). These proceedings discuss the completion of "the first contract utilizing the full failure-free warranty concept."

3. Robert K. Gates, John E. Bortz, and Robert S. Bickwell, "A Quantitative Analysis of Alternative RIW Implementations, *Proceedings of the IEEE 1976 National Aerospace and Electronics Conference* (NAECON 76) (Dayton, Ohio: Institute of Electrical and Electronics Engineers, 1976).

4. C. David Weimer, *The Impact of Reliability Guarantees and Warranties on Electronic Subsystem Design and Development Programs*, S-483 (Washington, D.C.: Institute for Defense Analyses, October 1976).

5. Ibid.

6. Teledyne Ryan Aeronautical, 56 Comp. Gen., B-187325,

April 20, 1977, provides a recent legal opinion. U.S., Department of Defense, "DOD Incentive Contracting Guide" (Washington, D.C.: Assistant Secretary of Defense [Installations and Logistics], 1965), provides an early but complete discussion of incentive contracting.

7. J. Michael Cummins, "Incentive Contracting for National Defense: A Problem of Optimal Risk Sharing," *Bell Journal of Economics* 8, no. 1 (Spring 1977).

8
Cost Models and Computers

Cost models are used to calculate LCC. This chapter is for the user of such models, the analyst who needs to provide an LCC estimate. It will not discuss the programming of the models for the computer; professional programmers must do this after the analyst decides what he wants the model to do and whether a computer would be desirable. The development of a new model may not be necessary if an existing model can be used. A comprehensive survey of existing computerized models has been compiled by the air force.[1] A description and evaluation of classes of models and an excellent bibliography make this report a substantial help in the selection of an appropriate model.

Simple cost models have been discussed in Chapters 2 and 4. The methods of estimating the costs to be inserted in the models—the CERs—have been discussed in Chapters 2 through 5. It may be useful here to start with a formal definition of cost models before describing them and discussing what features are most advantageous.

Definition of Cost Models

A cost model is a method, based on technical and programmatic parameters, of estimating costs. It converts the verbal

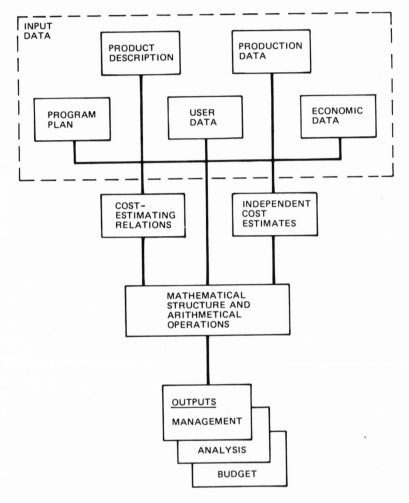

Figure 8-1. The Scope of a Cost Model

description of the program into a step-by-step procedure to calculate costs. Thus, a cost model can be defined in progressively broadening terms:

1. The mathematical structure describing how the LCC elements are summed is called an *accounting* model.

2. Addition of the cost-estimating relations for each element to the mathematical structure yields an *estimating* model. If it also includes discounting and inflation proce-

dures, it is an *economic* model.

3. Adding the data inputs, and if used, the computer programming, to the mathematical structure and the CERs provides a more completely scoped model. In this book, these are the essential features of the word *model* (see Figure 8-1).

4. We may expand the meaning of *model* to include the other models used with the LCC model, such as econometric models, and the people to operate them.

5. The broadest usage of *model* would incorporate the whole costing process, including management review actions and decisions.

In accordance with general usage, this book will use *model* as defined in (3) above. Note that other models may be part of the LCC process. For example, the optimum-repair-level analysis models (either manual, or computerized such as ORLA, LOCAM, or LORA) determine the best size for repair modules and the level at which they should be repaired.[2] Other models may be used to calculate maintenance manpower, inventory requirements (MOD METRIC), economic order quantities, or warranty provisions.[3] Separate econometric models provide data to the LCC model on economic factors such as inflation rates, labor costs, and cost of capital.[4] Conversely, it is possible to perform some of these computations by using sensitivity analysis methods (see below) in conjunction with parts of the LCC model.

Description of a Cost Model

Simple LCC accounting models sum costs to give an estimate of the total LCC only, but it is usually important to get the cost of the various subdivisions, too—for example, the cost of each phase or the contractor's costs. One of the most desirable features of the mathematical structure of a cost model is the ability to sum costs in various ways or "dimensions." Each dimension has a hierarchy of levels at which cost subtotals are of interest. In a complex model of three or more dimensions, such as Figure 4-2, and where the WBS dimension may have hundreds of subdivisions, the summing of several dimensions is much easier with a computer than with a manual model. The various possible dimensions of a cost model are:

1. Work breakdown structure as given in MIL-STD-881. This provides a hierarchal breakdown of the hardware delivered to the user and lists some of the user's costs.

2. Organizational subdivisions of work. These subdivisions make it possible to designate a responsible organization and individual in such areas as design, testing, manufacturing, inspection, tool design, and shipping.

3. Elements of cost. This categorizes costs as done by accounting organizations, e.g., direct material, direct labor, labor overhead, special testing, travel, and so on.

4. Program phase. This shows the sequence of program activities, e.g., conceptual, validation, full-scale development, production, and operation and maintenance.

5. Cost breakdown structure (CBS). The sample in Table 4-2 is adapted from the CBS used in the Navy Weapons Engineering Support Activity's LCC model. This structure relates elements of cost to program phase and subdivisions of work. It may facilitate separation of "contractor costs" from "government costs," even though some government costs may later be contracted out, e.g., depot maintenance or base security.

6. Appropriation code. When the Congress appropriates money for the DOD or other governmental agencies, it assigns funds to a number of categories, such as operation and maintenance; procurement; and research, development, test, and evaluation. Funds appropriated for one category may not be shifted to another (except as discussed in Chapter 1), so government decision makers need to know how costs are divided between these codes.

7. Time. The length of time during which costs are incurred is the most important item for budgeting purposes.

It may be defined in months, quarters, or years, using calendar or fiscal years.

The intersections of each of these dimensions are *cost elements*, the basic building blocks of the model. For example, a cost element might be described in the WBS as an amplifier circuit board in the radar transmitter; in the organizational subdivision of work, this cost element might be designated as testing; under elements of cost, this might be direct labor; and by program phase, it could be a production cost. This same cost element might be under acquisition of prime system in the cost breakdown structure, and the appropriation code could be shipbuilding and conversion; the time might be the first quarter of fiscal 1980. All of these dimensions together precisely define the place and significance of the cost element; this is the cost of direct labor to test the radar transmitter amplifier circuit board during acquisition of the prime system in the first quarter of 1980 using the shipbuilding and conversion funds. A model should be able to sum all of the costs in a dimension and to do this in a hierarchal order.

Each cost element in an estimating model may have a CER to calculate its value. Input data provide the parameter values for these CERs. For example, the CER for the circuit board could use the number of components and the power dissipation to determine the direct labor test cost. In other cases, a CER is not used, and the input data designate the value of the element directly; these are called "throughput," because they are unchanged by the model. Such throughput values might be used for a circuit board that has been tested by a subcontractor at a fixed price. The throughput cost element values may be used by the model elsewhere, however. The purchase price of the circuit board may be added to the costs of other hardware and used in the CER for, say, installation and assembly costs.

In some computer models, the analyst may change CERs by changing the input data. For even greater flexibility, the model's mathematical structure can be changed by using the input instructions; cost categories can be added or deleted, and even the output format can be changed. Such flexibility of course requires much more complex programming.

Model Structure

The architecture of the model, the way it is put together, is fundamental and will shape its subsequent use. Among the questions to be decided at this point are the relative independence of the various CERs (is the same value of the variable used in many CERs so that they are interdependent?). How many dimensions are to be accommodated? Is the model to be computerized? The use and format of the input data, the output format and its possible variations, the operation in a batch or interactive mode (if computerized), the size and kind of computer to use, or the capabilities of the people who will do the manual computations, the language of the model (equations can be written in English, algebra, or computer languages such as COBOL or FORTRAN), and so on are other problems. The details and implications of these issues will be discussed later. Suffice it to say that decisions on the above questions should be made when the model is being planned and not be made later by default because options were unintentionally foreclosed at an earlier date.

General Purpose vs. Special Purpose

Because programming is expensive, it is clearly more economical to use a general purpose model than to build a special purpose model for each program to be costed. In order to achieve generality, however, the model builder must often sacrifice specificity. Definitions become more diffuse; the models grow to include all possible cost categories; and the CERs add terms to include all possible circumstances. Yet the attractiveness of a limited number of general purpose models persists. As the state of the art develops, it may be possible to devise widely usable general structures and to modify their internal workings to suit particular applications. At present, most analysts either prepare a new model for each program or adapt an old model for the particular characteristics of the new program.

Deterministic or Probabilistic Models

A deterministic model produces a single output figure for a given set of input figures. If the internal workings of the model allow for variable outputs due to measures of risk or calculation methods, then the model is probabilistic. The calculation method may be probabilistic if it is not possible to state the cost relations explicitly in an equation. An implicit equation requires a number of trials, using various values to approximate the solution; the solution then depends on the number of trials and on the initial estimate. The use of many trials with random numbers as input values is called a Monte Carlo method and is the most common probabilistic calculation method.

Because all cost estimates are uncertain, a model may accept the input values as a probability distribution to use in determining the possible variability of the final output. The output of a probabilistic model output provides a more complete understanding than that of a deterministic model, but its variable output is harder to understand, it is more costly to set up and operate, and its answer is often unwelcome. Few managers want to tell their supervision or their customer that a project is risky or an estimate uncertain. Thus, although it is possible to construct probabilistic models that are intellectually satisfying and mathematically rigorous, most LCC models are deterministic.[5]

CERs Based on Performance or Physical Characteristics

In developing CERs, the initial attempts were to use the

performance characteristics (speed, accuracy, effectiveness, kill probability, range, data capacity, and load) as measures of cost. As noted in earlier chapters, this has not always explained cost relationships (in fact, often no relation could be found). Many newer CERs are based on physical hardware characteristics (weight, volume, material, and complexity). The RCA PRICE model is based on the latter type of CER and has been highly successful in predicting costs.

The PRICE model was formulated as a universal system to generate appropriate regressions or CERs for a range of products or systems. In essence, it peforms a multidimensional extrapolation of past experience to predict cost. Since all products must have weight and size, these are used by PRICE as the principal descriptors. Electronic equipments are characterized by the kind of components and circuits used. Mechanical structures are described in terms of types of materials, construction, and densities. In addition, certain PRICE inputs describe the way an organization operates— its way of doing business. Thus, the model can be adapted to reflect appropriate cost element definitions.

Early in the program, systems engineers provide specifications for performance requirements. The translation of performance requirements into hardware descriptions is the designer's task; when it is necessary to obtain hardware descriptions for input to a model, the designers, not the cost analysts, should do the translation. If this is not possible, performance-type CERs may be used if available. A model should generally be restricted to either the performance or the hardware type of CER. A mix of the two types increases the input data requirements and may even produce internally inconsistent results.

When developing a CER, check the correlation coefficient of the completed equation. A low correlation may indicate an unsatisfactory CER. Check also the limits of the range of input variables for which the CER seems to work.

Desirable Features of Models

There are many desirable features of a model, but some of these can be mutually contradictory, e.g., simplicity and comprehensiveness. Finding an adequate compromise tests the skill of the model designer. The following list should be considered in designing a model, along with the suggestions for achieving these features.

Economy. A model should be cheap to develop, to alter, to provide with data (it should not be costly to change the data), and to operate. These cost considerations include labor costs, computer costs, and acquisition costs of computer programs, data, or other purchased materials. A simple model, using only the significant cost drivers, is the goal. The CERs should be simple, linear, explicit calculations, not recursive loops that require repeated operations.

Speed. It should be possible to set up, operate, and change a model quickly. Speed is important to the users of the output. A manual model, using paper and pencils, not computers, is particularly apt for small tasks. The analyst can do the job alone instead of waiting for programmers, computer time, or the resolution of administrative delays. Even though computers are fast, programmers and administrators can be slow. The data required should be easily available and minimal. The input data format should be simple and easy to understand; it will be easier to make changes if the input data can be processed in random order.

Ease of operation. To be economical and fast, a model must be easy to operate. It should be usable by designers and other technical personnel, as well as by LCC specialists. A standardized model eliminates the need to retrain personnel for each new project. The use of default values for missing or unknown parameters can be very helpful; default values provide nominal figures that the model can use for a parameter when no value has been supplied. The nominal default value may be good for most cases but very wrong for some, and all users should be cautioned. Another attractive feature for ease of operation is the ability to input values at various levels of the hierarchical structure of a dimension. For example, if the WBS is detailed to the fourth level, but some data are available only to the third level, it should be possible to input data at either the third or the fourth level. Finally, the input values should be used by the model directly; the analyst should not have to resort to some code book to translate values into computer language. Computers do this translation more easily.

Program and design sensitivity. The model should clearly show the cost impact of design and program characteristics. This is particularly true of the CERs. For example, a production CER should be sensitive to the material used and the schedule required. All too often, for the sake of simplicity, CERs assume conventional materials and reasonable schedules. The naive user may input data for exotic materials or unreasonable schedules and get misleading results. As another example, the CERs of the model should be sensitive to the cost implications of the choice between built-in test equipment and external support equipment. Such a decision has effects on all phases of a program. This sensitivity in the model will make it possible to answer "what if" questions with sensible cost results.

Feasible data requirements. The CERs and the model should only require available data. To accomplish this, the model may be tailored to work with known significant historical data. The user should be able to concentrate on getting the few items of data peculiar to the particular program; he should not waste time gathering data that will not materially influence the output or that is repetitive from program to program. For example, CERs for transportation and travel costs often require detailed information on future plans but change costs by less than 1 percent. Such costs can be approximated or, better, omitted.

The model should minimize the task of manipulating the data. For example, the same datum should not have to be entered more than once. Data should be accepted in a variety of forms—e.g., it should be possible to express time in either hours, minutes, and seconds, or in hours and decimal fractions of hours. If more than one value of a datum is used, the computer should accept only the last value or, perhaps, calculate the average of all values input. Some models even upgrade the data inputs, invalidating the old saw of "garbage in, garbage out"; the data enhancement is achieved by comparing different parameters and advising if they are not consistent with usual practice. For example, the model might calculate the payload fraction of a bomber or truck and advise of a fatal error if it was not less than 1 (as it physically must be) and of a nonfatal error if it did not fall within the usual limits of, say, 0.6 to 0.8.

Economic capability and flexibility. Economic models should provide a discounting method with the rate to be selected by the analyst. The inflation rate should also be selected by the user. A built-in inflation table should be available as a default value (see Chapter 6 for details).

Variable learning curves. Because learning curves in various types of manufacturing differ widely, the model should accept various slopes. These learning curves (see Chapter 3) should be applicable to manufacturing costs, maintenance costs, and operating costs.

Ease of transition to detailed quotation. After completion of the LCC estimate, a customer, e.g., the Congress, may require the submission of a detailed quotation. The customer usually mandates the format of the quotation, and the model output should easily fit into that format.

Usefulness throughout a program. The model should be usable throughout the life cycle of a program. The various hierarchies such as the WBS and CERs should be expandable to accommodate the growing complexity of a program as it proceeds. The model should be no more complex than is needed at any given time. Note that programmers must revise the program periodically, and they cost money.

Tolerance and helpfulness. The model should be tolerant of input errors. Some models will accept only input values within a limited range, advising the user to correct deviant values; preferably the model merely warns the user of an errant value and continues the job. Most computer models provide error messages if there are problems in the input; these messages should be as explicit as possible. The messages should be categorized as either "fatal," e.g., "the allowable array size has been exceeded and the run is aborted," or "non-fatal," e.g., "(name) is an invalid variable name, and the run will omit that variable." It should be possible to add explanatory notes and comments to the output format.

Performance of sensitivity analyses. The capability to vary one or more parameters over a range is valuable. If the model can divide the range of a variable provided by the user into, say, ten steps and then give an LCC estimate for each step while holding all other inputs constant, the user can see the impact of that particular variable. The size of the operating crew, for example, enters into a number of CERs, and the user may find it helpful to see the change in the LCC with changes in the crew size. Even more useful is the model's ability to generate LCC estimates for two correlated parameters that vary simultaneously. For example, if the reliability of an item varies with the purchase price, a sensitivity analysis could show if a minimum LCC exists as a function of the reliability and price. The model might even provide an output graph.

Modular format. A modular program is easier to repair and to modify, and the separate modules are economical to run for special purposes. During the development of the model, it is useful to be able to assign the separate modules to different programmers. A modular program is separated into a number of relatively independent sections (modules), which can be calculated independently. For example, a module might be used to calculate operating personnel costs. When the module has been completed, the value obtained can be used in another module that calculates all operational costs.

Security. A model should be secure against unauthorized access to the information by commercial interests or other parties seeking classified military data. The use of computers for cryptanalysis has tended to make security a relative matter, so that a highly secure code is one that requires large resources and a long time to decipher; a simple code can be broken with limited resources in a short time. The user of a model should also guard against the inadvertent loss or destruction of the model—e.g., fire—or the modification of the model—e.g., computer memory errors.

Inclusiveness. The model should include all significant costs and influences on costs. For example, if there is a change from an armored division to an airborne division, or from the army to the navy, is the cost impact discernible? Are software costs included? In estimating the LCC of airborne missiles, the cost of the launch aircraft is usually omitted. Yet in a recent problem where two proposed missiles were to be compared, the launch aircraft attrition rate was thought to be different. Inclusion of the launch aircraft costs made a decisive change in the estimate. On the other hand, for reasons of economy, do not include insignificant costs merely for the sake of completeness or to avoid criticism. Excessive complexity may obscure the small, significant set of parameters that have a pivotal impact on the results.

Authoritativeness. The model should be accepted by management and the customer as authoritative. Its accuracy should have been validated; the origin of all CERs should be traceable; and the input data should be justifiable. The inputs and the outputs should be terms familiar to the users so that they can evaluate their reasonableness by experience.

Now, how can all of these requirements be embodied in a usable model? The first decision to be made is whether to use a manual or a computer model.

Manual Model or Computer Model?

If the model has a small number of cost elements and if the LCC estimate is to be done only a few times, a manual procedure is recommended. The only benefit of a computer in these cases would be to add to the LCC mystique. Larger efforts or repetitious ones probably justify the time and expense of a computer program. A deterrent to a computer model is the time and expense required for programming; even for a simple model, this may take several weeks. Only parts of the model may be computerized for use in a small hand-held or desk-top calculator. For example, programs for such portable calculators on minimizing provisioning cost have proved valuable at provisioning conferences. Most participants can offer only intuitive judgment, but the calculator carries the authority of mathematics. For major LCC estimates with a WBS of more than fifty categories and at least two other dimensions, a large computer is very helpful in keeping the data orderly and is also faster, cheaper, and more flexible than manual methods. Lastly, computers are less likely than people to make transcription errors, calculation errors, or procedural errors.

Computer Characteristics

Computers can handle and manipulate large amounts of data economically. The large data processing machines, such as the IBM 370, are used primarily for business applications, such as LCC, while other machines, such as the CDC 6400, are used mainly for scientific applications. The scientific machines are often distinguished by their use of larger word size for increased precision. Many computers have an interactive mode, where the operator provides data and instructions at a console and the computer responds immediately. Many analysts find the interactive mode helpful for cost-trade studies and sensitivity analyses because they can immediately see the results and try various approaches to the problem. Most LCC work on a computer requires large amounts of input data, however, and generates correspondingly large amounts of output. For this work, the batch mode is recommended. In the batch mode the complete input data file is assembled on cards or tape and is read into the machine memory. After the entire program has been calculated and stored in memory, the computer prints out the results. One organization has found that the ideal mix of batch and interactive computing uses (1) batch initially to input the data, (2) interactive manipulation of these data for various "what if" studies, and (3) batch output reporting for the final report.

An average-size LCC program (the Naval Weapons Engineering Support Activity model) requires about 320 K bytes (8 bits = 1 byte) of memory. The Air Force Logistic Command's Logistic Support Cost model requires about a third of that. These memory requirements put such programs near the maximum capability of even large desk-top machines, such as the Hewlitt Packard 9815, and are usually run on larger machines (which are also faster).

Business programs are more conveniently written in COBOL; FORTRAN is usually used for scientific calculations. LCC models share some characteristics of both business and scientific computations. For this reason, the programmer's preference or convenience is most likely to determine the choice of computer language.

Output Formats

The first rule is "know thy customer." The output must be suited to the user. Busy, upper level executives want a brief summary of the LCC estimate, as in Figure 8-2. Even this may be too detailed, and briefing charts may be extracts of this material, as shown in Figure 8-3. The summary matrix should have no more than ten columns or rows. A number of matrices may be provided, in addition to the phase vs. cost

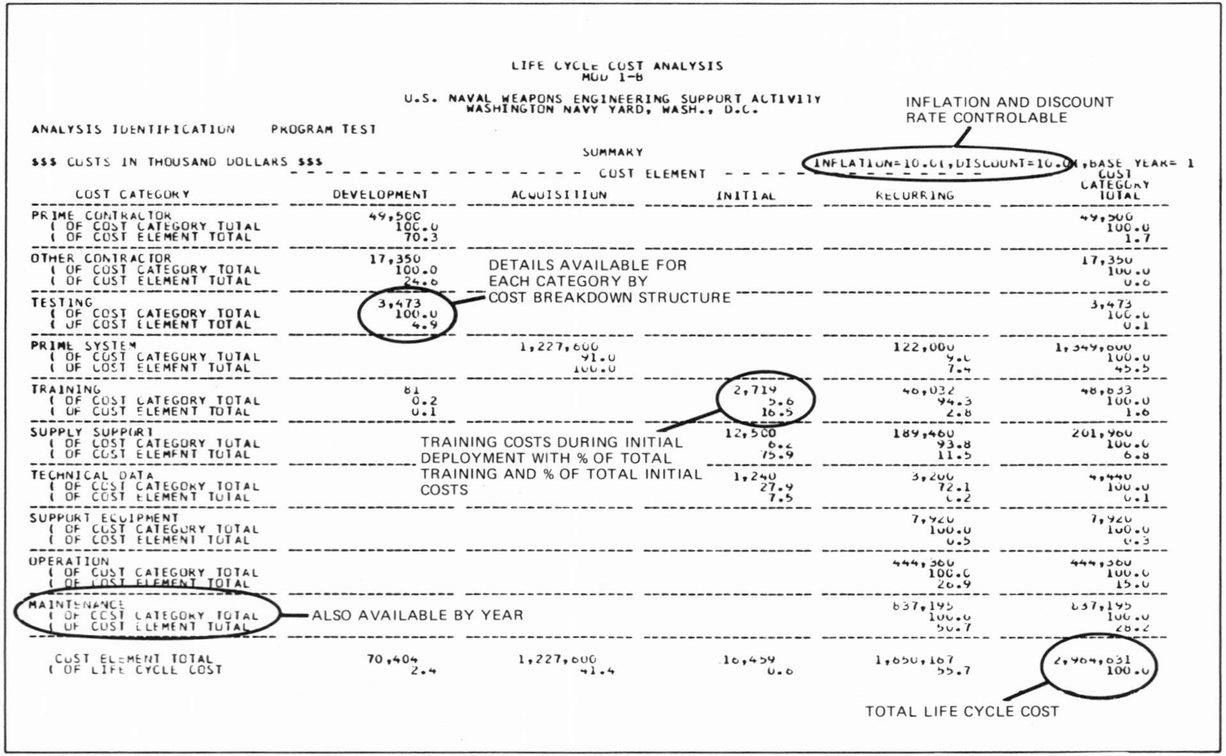

Figure 8-2. LCC Model Summary Output

L I F E   C Y C L E   C O S T

	Base Program	Alternate I	Difference
DEVELOPMENT	$$$,$$$	$$$,$$$	$$,$$$
PRODUCTION	$$$,$$$	$$$,$$$	$$,$$$
OPERATION AND SUPPORT	$$$,$$$	$$$,$$$	$$,$$$
TOTAL	$,$$$,$$$	$,$$$,$$$	$$$,$$$

Figure 8 –3. Simplified Briefing Chart

breakdown structure, using time, appropriation code, elements of cost, or other dimensions. Each should be on one page, suitable for direct reproduction in a report.

At the next level of detail, a set of no more than ten sheets explains the summary sheets. It should be easy to trace a value in the summary back to the details. At all levels, per-centages provide a quick understanding of the relative impor-tance of each number. Note in Figure 8-2 that each value is accompanied by its percentage of its row and its column.

Keep in mind that graphic presentations, bar charts, and line graphs may be clearer to many individuals than numbers alone; the computer can be programmed to produce such dis-plays, as in Figure 8-4, even without a plotter. Figure 8-4 could be expanded into a cost profile, showing the cost of each year of the life cycle.

The analyst will want a far more detailed output than his customers do. The value of each cost element, showing the output of the CER, should be listed in sequence. A listing of all inputs, by code, provides reassurance that the program understood the intended values. For even more help, the code for each input can be translated into plain English. Other outputs can provide costs with and without inflation and/or discounting factors. The results of sensitivity analyses should be presented in tabular and graphic formats so that they will be readily usable in reports.

The user should be able to select the outputs desired at various levels of detail. Do not force him to wade through many pages to find such information. Computers are good at rearranging data and should be used for it.

Programming and Programmers

This discussion for the model user assumes that a profes-sional computer programmer will be engaged when a decision is made to use a computer. (Computer specialists would prefer to be consulted before that decision, but remember that they are likely to favor the use of computers.) Because the task of designing or modifying a model is so complex, communication between programmer and model developer should be in writing. The importance of a disciplined, orderly mode of communication between them cannot be overem-

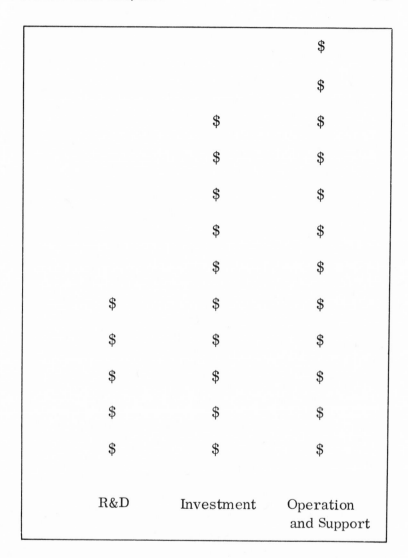

Figure 8 -4. Graphical Computer Output

phasized. Of course, regular, face-to-face discussions are necessary, too, and mutual trust and understanding are vital. But adequate documentation to describe what is wanted and what has been delivered is just as important, especially to those who will follow in later years.

The model developer might start by summarizing for the programmer the desired features, as discussed earlier in this chapter. The formal request for a new or modified program should be embodied in a computer program performance specification; the user prepares this specification (after discussions with the programmer). The programming organization will develop a number of internal documents for its own guidance. At the completion of the project, the programmer should provide:

1. a user's manual, which might be drafted by the user and then revised by the programmer to reflect the resultant program
2. a computer program operator's manual
3. a computer program test plan and procedures

A typical specification describing these documents is the navy's WS-8506.[6] Philip Metzger's comprehensive analysis of the whole process of developing a program includes a worthwhile procedure for the formal acceptance of the program at completion.[7]

Programming and Computer Costs

Chapter 2 proposed a very simple CER for programming costs. Clearly, there are many more variables involved than that simple three-factor equation allows. In the RCA PRICE model, thousands of instructions are required to write the algorithm for estimating programming costs. A number of references are available for such comprehensive estimates. The recommended procedure is to request an estimate from a programming group (the bottom up method). Do not forget the cost of maintaining the program after it has been written. For example, on navy tactical computer systems, one full-time programmer is required for software maintenance for each 32K of core memory.

Similarly, the cost of operating a large computer is approximately $600 per hour. This charge varies with the amount of memory used, the amount of input and output data, the central processor time, additional supplies, keypunch operators' time, and any other support personnel needed.

Future Developments

The ability of a model to obtain some of its inputs from another existing model is an exciting development that is now being explored. For example, many firms have the complete bill of materials for a system, sometimes with price and weight data, on a computer memory. Clearly, the LCC model needs much of this data. A method of linking computer programs would relieve much of the input data work load.

It would be very useful if effectiveness models could also be linked with LCC models to share input data and, more importantly, to obtain outputs in terms of optimum LCC. This would mechanize the cost-effectiveness analysis problem at a more complete level than is common today. Some form of linear programming[8] or other method of mathematical programming could be used. This idea is clearly within the scope of the technical performance measurement requirement of the military systems engineering specification.[9] The combined effectiveness and LCC program would include risk analysis, schedule, mission requirements analysis, production methods and rates, availability, and so on to implement the technical performance measurement.

As noted earlier, the data required for inputs to LCC models are sorely lacking. The agencies that collect such data are improving their analysis of the information, and the user may eventually be able to choose among a variety of data products, all in a machine-accessible form that could be used directly in an LCC model without the intermediate step of a keypunch operator. With further progress (and demand), the data might be made available on a real-time basis, so that an LCC model would be current as new data become available. Such current data might include reliability, maintainability, acquisition costs, installation costs, depot costs (especially overhead), change incorporation and configuration control, and labor rates.

Finally, models need to be simplified, separating the significant few costs from the trivial many.

Summary

1. A model is made up of a mathematical structure, CERs, discounting and inflation procedures, data, and, if used, a computer program.

2. Cost models have a number of dimensions, and the intersections are the cost elements.

3. The value of the cost elements is obtained by CERs or is given by the input data directly (throughput).

4. The user of a model must decide if a new model is required and what characteristics that model should have. An important decision is whether to use a computer.

5. Communications with programmers should be documented.

Notes

1. Dwight E. Collins, *Analysis of Available Life Cycle Cost Models and Their Applications,* Joint AFSC/AFLC Commanders' Working Group on Life Cycle Cost, ASD/ACL, Wright-Patterson Air Force Base, Ohio, June 1976.

2. These terms are acronyms: optimum-repair-level analysis (ORLA) and level-of-repair analysis (LORA) are essentially the same process; logistics cost analysis model (LOCAM) is an army computer program that does level-of-repair analysis.

3. John A. Muckstadt and John M. Pearson, "MOD METRIC: A Multi-Echelon, Multi-Indenture Inventory

Model," Air Force Logistics Command, Wright-Patterson Air Force Base, Ohio, June 1972.

4. The Wharton School of Finance, Philadelphia, Pa., the University of California at Los Angeles, Los Angeles, Calif., and the Federal Reserve Bank of the United States, Washington, D.C., periodically provide the results of their econometric models.

5. Howard Raiffa and Robert Schlaiffer, *Applied Statistical Decision Theory* (Cambridge, Mass.: Harvard University Press, 1961); Gerald A. Fleischer, ed., *Risk and Uncertainty: Non-Deterministic Decision Making in Engineering Economy* (Norcross, Ga.: Engineering Economy Division, American Institute of Industrial Engineers, 1975).

6. U.S. Navy, *Requirements for Digital Computer Program Documentation,* WS-8506, (Washington D.C.: Department of the Navy, n.d.).

7. Philip W. Metzger, *Managing a Programming Project* (Englewood Cliffs, N.J.: Prentice-Hall, 1973).

8. Hamdy A. Taha, *Operations Research: An Introduction* (New York: Macmillan, 1971).

9. U.S. Air Force, *Engineering Management,* MIL-STD-499A (USAF) (Washington, D.C., 1974). A complete discussion of this specification is in Chapter 9.

9
The Development Process

The effectiveness of an LCC program is measured by its impact on the system under consideration. LCC must change the configuration of the system, its design, or the way it is produced or used. The federal government has mandated such cost-performance interaction in the OMB Bulletin A-109,[1] which states that systems should be procured with adequate performance at an affordable price. (In England, the government has promoted a similar idea as "terotechnology." See the Glossary.) To accomplish this, the planning and designing team must determine what the customer's cost goals are and how important they are in relation to performance, schedule, and other values. Bulletin A-109 encourages program developers to challenge cost and other goals and to have them changed if such action will reduce LCC. The determination and implementation of such values is the business of the development process.

This chapter will analyze ways in which LCC can shape the development process so as to reduce costs. From a costing point of view, the vital development methods are system engineering, cost trade-offs, reliability, maintainability, safety, design to cost, logistics, and, of course, design. System engineering starts the development process and integrates LCC with the other disciplines. So as to be able to work effectively with system engineering, all LCC analysts should understand the process used.

System Engineering

System engineering transforms an operational need (mission requirement) into a description of system performance parameters (design requirements) and a preferred system configuration.[2] To do this, a plan is needed, alternative system configurations must be compared on a cost and effectiveness basis, and a method of measuring technical performance must be available. The following description portrays an idealized complete process, even though shortcuts may be taken.

As shown in Figure 9-1, system engineering receives the customer requirements and performs a mission analysis, synthesizing a conceptual arrangement of the required functions (Figure 9-2), which must be performed to achieve the desired result. Note that the analyst should be concerned at this stage with functions, not mechanisms, and should be aware of the constraints within which the system will operate. OMB Bulletin A-109, for example, explains how to draw up a "Mission Element Need Statement" that will systematically develop the set of capabilities required within such constraints as the physical laws controlling the system. The cost analyst should then allocate the various requirements, including cost, to the sequence of functions (Figure 9-3). For some analysts, this may be a new and unusual task. Rather than costing a known hardware item such as a missile, or even a task such as a flight test, it may be necessary to cost a seemingly nonspecific "delivery system with a 5,000-kilometer range and a payload of 100 kilograms." Estimating the cost of any single function may be so difficult that the cost analyst may instead divide what the customer indicates is the "affordable cost" of the entire system among the various functions in some arbitrary way. Later cost estimates

183

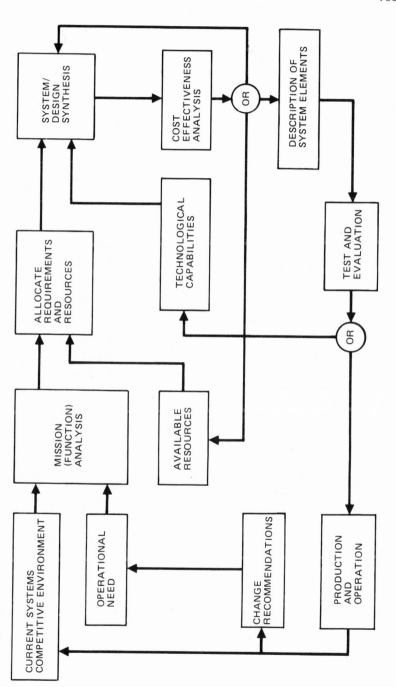

Figure 9-1. The System Engineering Process

Figure 9-2.   Conceptual Phase Functional Flow

will determine whether the functions can be mechanized for that estimate. The effort not to exceed a target cost will tax the designers' ingenuity (see below under *design to cost*). A more sophisticated technique would be to assign each function a target cost with a range of variability. This variability is shown in Figure 9-3.

As the system engineers define the system's functions in more detail, perhaps changing it on the basis of the cost and schedule information provided above, they should prepare new functional flows and more refined estimates of the more detailed functions. Beware of the temptation to assume that there is only one way of accomplishing the function. Try to postpone the choice of method until several ways of carrying out a function have been proposed. Each one, along with its costs and schedules, can then be evaluated, using the methods discussed in Chapters 2 through 5. If none of the proposed solutions meets the requirements, the system engineer may try to find a more advantageous means of meeting the customer's need, or it may be necessary to reconsider the available resources in the light of the impasse. This early consideration of the cost for all phases of the program (LCC) provides the foundation for a satisfactory LCC effort during the remaining stages of system development. Furthermore, such early cost analysis can contribute significantly to the acceptance of the program by the customer and his management and by the

185

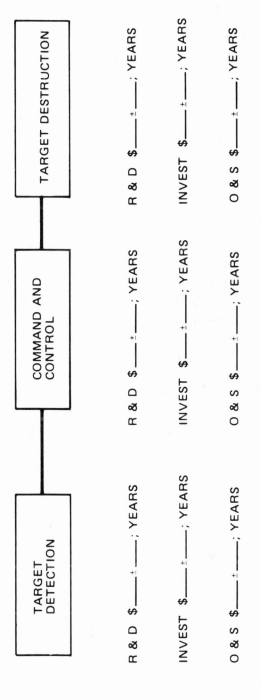

Figure 9-3. Functional Flow With Cost Estimate, Range and Schedule

Congress. All customers are reassured when shown that their costs are being considered and controlled.

After the satisfactory completion of this cost-effectiveness analysis, the next step is to prepare a detailed description of the system (the design), and to build and test prototypes. If these meet the operational needs, they should be produced and operated. From these operations, new needs will be perceived and changes recommended, starting the process again.

System Engineering Plan

The system engineering process, described above, is sufficiently complex and costly to warrant a formal plan, such as the manufacturing or logistics plans. In Military Standard 499A, this is called a System Engineering Management Plan. The plan should initially outline the work to be done and describe the schedule in sufficient detail to estimate the cost of the plan. As the program progresses, the plan will accumulate details. Three major sections are recommended:

1. *Technical program planning and control.* This section should identify organizational responsibilities, levels, and methods of control for performance and design requirements; program reviews; and documentation control. It should include a technical performance measurement system as described below.

2. *System engineering process.* This section should describe the process (see Figure 9-1), the trade study methodology (see below), the mathematical and/or simulation models to be used for system and cost-effectiveness evaluation, and the method of developing specifications.

3. *Engineering specialty integration.* This section should focus on ways to coordinate the work of various engineering specialties, such as integrated logistics support, test engineering, production engineering, transportability, reliability, maintainability, safety engineering, standardization, design to cost, and life cycle cost. The system engineering process must

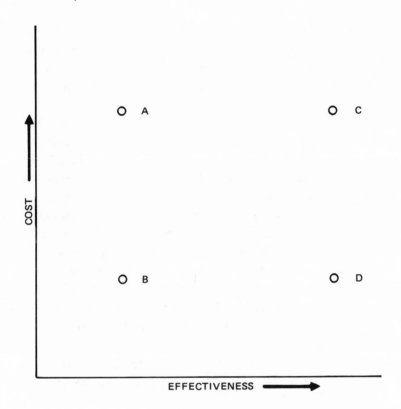

Figure 9-4. Cost and Effectiveness Comparison

find ways to integrate and harmonize the separate concerns of each of these specialties, neither exaggerating nor neglecting any of them, so that the best possible design results.

System Comparisons

During the cost-effectiveness analysis, it is easy to compare and to choose between two systems of equal performance and different costs. In Figure 9-4, system *B* clearly dominates sytem *A*, and *D* dominates *C*. It is also easy to compare and to choose between systems that cost the same but perform differently. The choice becomes more difficult, however, when the system with the better performance (*C*) is also more expensive than the alternative (*B*). In such cases, it may be possible to compare the alternatives by normalizing the performance differences for cost differences. For example, if system *C* is a bomber that is more expensive but carries a greater payload than bomber *B*, the LCC estimate could be divided by the payload capabilities to obtain a cost per pound of payload. This cost per pound of payload—the *figure of merit*—can be used to compare the two systems. Similarly, payload differences in missiles, cargo carriers, and guns can be compared. Many other performance parameters cannot be so handled if the performance measure is highly nonlinear. For instance, the maximum speed of an aircraft is significant in relation to the speed of potential enemy fighters. If the aircraft is slower than the attacking fighter, the degree of difference is less important than its evasive maneuverability relative to the attacker. Furthermore, the range and speed of its air-to-air missiles may determine the outcome of the engagement. Clearly, these are nonlinear relations, and the function that measures "effectiveness" or "performance" must be carefully crafted.

The use of LCC analysis for design trade-offs implies that all values can be quantified in money terms. Many system characteristics cannot be evaluated in dollars, however. Availability, surprise, public opinion, environmental degradation, destabilization of international relations, and loss of life do not convert into money in any simple way. But they all are important in the decision-making process that is LCC's reason for being. The LCC analyst should understand and recognize such residual differences between alternative competitive proposals after he has attempted to price as many of the differences as possible. The LCC analysis should include footnotes, much like an auditor's opinion, to explain the noncostable differences.

All products, all systems interface with other products and systems; these interfacing systems may be complex man-

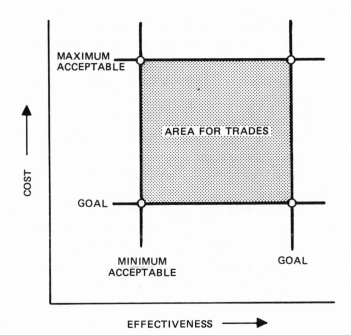

Figure 9-5. Cost and Effectiveness Trade-offs

machine aggregations, such as a naval carrier task force or a highway system, or simple mechanical interfaces such as a pipe thread. If the new product under consideration requires a change in the "external" interfacing system, the costs of that change must also be considered in the LCC estimate.

Cost-Effectiveness Trade-off Bounds

The concept of cost and effectiveness illustrated in Figure 9-4 may be carried somewhat further, as shown in Figure 9-5. Here, the minimum effectiveness acceptable to the customer is shown, with an effectiveness goal; a maximum affordable cost is also shown, with a desired cost goal. These define an area within which the developer may propose cost and effectiveness trade-offs. Designs falling outside of this area are considered unacceptable by the customer. The DOD is using such "floor" and "target" requirements to define the latitude available to the developer in cost and effectiveness.

An important aspect of system synthesis is the use of existing designs, modified if necessary, as part of the new system. Existing designs in the user's inventory offer a number of advantages:

1. No design or development work is necessary.

2. It is easy to introduce the design into the user's environment because there is no need to provide extra training, new facilities, new logistics planning, new technical manuals, new support equipment, or new provisioning.

3. The use of an existing design, with a known cost and performance, involves fewer risks than the development and deployment of a new system. The cost advantage of such risk reduction is highly significant, for most new systems must allow at least 20 percent for possible cost overruns in their budget.

Technical Performance Measurement

As stated earlier, part of the program planning and control method is a technical performance measurement to monitor progress and detect problems in meeting operational needs. This requires a definition of the critical parameters of the operational need, for example, speed, schedule, or production cost. Moreover, an evaluation of the risk in meeting these critical parameters will assist in focusing attention on the sensitive issues. With these highlighted, a tracking system can be initiated to monitor the current estimates of each parameter. Such a technical performance measurement (TPM) system is suggested by MIL-STD-499. This measurement system must simulate the operation of the entire system being developed as the data available during development show details of each component. The TPM must combine this detail data to predict the characteristics of the system when completed. The output of this system simulation is then compared with the desired values of the critical parameters determined earlier. Note that the TPM simulation should include costs and schedules of the system. As the system is defined in greater detail, the TPM should follow the work breakdown structure (WBS), with performance requirements, cost estimates, and schedules for each WBS item. Here, again, the process may require allocating and estimating costs, changing the design or the allocation if there is a difference between the allocation and estimate, and starting again.

The logistic support analysis should start concurrently with the system development. This analysis, discussed in Chapter 4, depicts the support functions necessary to achieve the required operational capability and follows closely the methods used in the operational function flow diagram (Figure 9-6). Costs and schedule should be assigned to each support function, and the logistics system engineer should follow the same process of successively detailing and refining the diagram; evaluating the feasibility of each step within the price, schedule, and doctrinal constraints; and inventing new support methods or reallocating costs and schedules where conflicts develop. The term *schedule* used here means both the development time to get the system in place and the time required to perform the function (time-line analysis) during operations. Simultaneously, while the systems engineers are allocating the performance requirements (e.g., weight, miss distance, reliability, maintainability, and fuel consumption) to the lower equipment levels, they should consider the allocated logistics requirements. The reliability and maintainability requirements may be modified, or new design requirements on standardization, mobility, or endurance may be imposed. With such efforts, the logistics and technical requirements are integrated into an effective system.

Trade-offs

Each consideration of alternative designs requires the

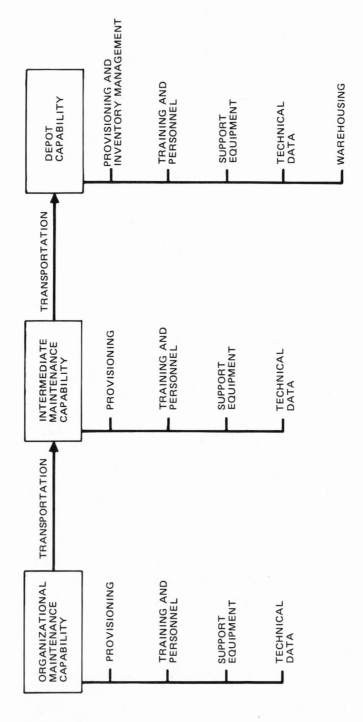

Figure 9-6. Support Functions Flow Diagram

analysis of possible trade-offs between competing values. Such analysis may involve formal, documented presentations that show the cost, performance, and schedule of each of a number of alternatives, or, when less information is available, it may only include a sensitivity analysis showing how a change in one parameter will change costs. If still less information is available, a simple ranking of the cost-sensitive issues can show the cost drivers. Another, older form of trade-off is the break-even analysis (see below). Those trade-offs that work across more than one phase of the life cycle are of particular concern to LCC analysis. They usually involve an increase in cost in the early phases in order to save money in later phases (on rare occasions, one might find ways of decreasing costs in the early phases with little cost penalty in the later operating and support phase). Although most examples of trade-offs have to do with high-level, "important" problems, the same methods are applicable at all levels. Both designers and system engineers use them, though the designers may omit the formal documentation. The line between system engineers and designers is defined by the level of control used by the customer. System engineers normally are responsible for synthesizing the system to the level of the customer's formal specifications. Designers generally see to it that the design synthesis meets the customer's formal specifications.

Even a simple design task, such as a cover plate, should yield trade-offs. The cover plate design can involve the decision among a number of choices, such as (1) a heavy cover plate with a few large screws holding it, (2) a lightweight cover plate with more and smaller screws, (3) a plate fastened with a number of quarter-turn fasteners, and (4) a fabricated plate with a thicker edge using either fewer quarter-turn fasteners or screws. The unit production costs of these alternatives must be considered, as well as any differences in design time and cost; above these, the user's time in opening and closing the cover should be evaluated. These costs, though small, span the research and development phase, the investment phase, and the operating and support phase.

In large complex systems, a significant trade-off concerns the division of work between the computer and other parts of the system, such as the radar—the "hardware vs. software" debate. Should the radar be designed with specialized circuits to interpret incoming information, or should the data be sent to the general purpose computer for processing and interpretation? Trade-off studies of the question frequently emphasize development and production costs and omit the cost of the inevitable later changes during the operational phase. This omission distorts the results of the trade-off study, because it costs less to change the software than it does to change the radar hardware. From an LCC point of view, an increased emphasis on the use of the computer with its flexible software seems desirable.

Sensitivity Analysis

If the input data used in calculating a cost trade-off are uncertain, how sensitive is the conclusion to changes in the input data? If an equation is available for the trade-off, it is clear that terms that are raised to a power are more influential than linear terms. Equations with differences in the denominator can show spectacular changes as the differences approach zero.

In the section on War Reserves in Chapter 4, the amount of ammunition needed was traded off against kill probability. The conclusion was that the higher of the two kill probabilities was desirable if more than 172 weapons were produced. The equations involved illustrate the sensitive parameters.

The total cost equation was:

Total Cost Change = (number of weapons fielded) x (cost per
weapon) + (fixed cost of change) − (number of
weapons fielded) x (ammunition cost saving)

where

Cost of improvement per weapon	$ 50,000
Ammunition cost saving due to the improvement	$ 79,200
Fixed cost of the change	$5,000,000

To find the break-even point in the number of weapons fielded, set the total cost change equal to zero (the change makes no difference):

$$0 = \text{(number of weapons fielded)} \times (50,000 + 5,000,000)$$
$$- \text{(number of weapons fielded)} \times (79,200)$$

or

$$\text{Number of weapons fielded} = \frac{5,000,000}{79,200 - 50,000} = 172$$

This states that if 172 weapons are fielded, the costs for the two alternative kill probabilities are equal. It also shows that as savings in ammunition due to the improvement approach the cost of improvement per weapon, the break-even point can rise sharply. If the value of either of the two variables is uncertain and only about 172 weapons are involved, it would not do to make very strong recommendations about the decision. On the other hand, if plans call for fielding many thousands of weapons, quite confident statements can be made.

Break-even Analysis

In the comparison of competing alternatives, another method used is the break-even analysis. For many years financial analysis usually included a calculation of the length

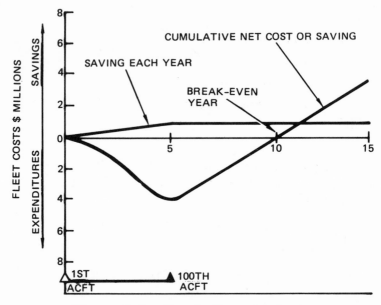

Figure 9-7. Break-Even Analysis
(Shows the Time for Operating Costs to Balance
Initial Costs)

of time required to recover the original investment, the break-even point. This has largely been supplanted by present value calculations, but break-even analysis is attractive because of its simplicity. An example of break-even analysis for a fighter aircraft (Figure 9-7) shows front-end costs of a change balanced against out-year savings. The break-even year came out to be ten years after the start of production. If the expected life of the fighter is at least ten years and if management is willing to wait ten years for a return on investment, the change under consideration should be approved.

Present Value

A present value approach to the last problem would discount the flow of savings and costs to the present time, using an appropriate discount rate (see Chapter 6). Management would then have a more rational basis for deciding whether it was willing to wait ten years for a return on investment. In this example, the schedule of net costs was:

Cost per year   = $1.18 million
Savings per year = $0.75 million for the 100-aircraft
                    fleet

In Table 9-1, discounting delays profit on the investment until the fifteenth year. In other words, the planned fleet life must be more than fifteen years if the present value of the change is to be positive. In such circumstances, most managements would reject the change.

Cost Drivers

To focus trade-offs on the important areas, the cost drivers must be known. Pareto's law (freely translated) states that most of the costs of a product are concentrated in a few parts of that product. For example, of 354 parts on the F-16 airplane, 50 accounted for 82 percent of the total cost. More generally, a few of the design-controllable system characteristics have a predominant effect on the LCC. Those of interest are the parameters that the program planners, system engineers, and designers can change while still meeting the user's needs. If attention can be concentrated on the few significant cost drivers, an efficient LCC program is possible. Uncontrollable costs, such as headquarters staff manpower, should be ignored.

Some common-sense, general ideas seem obvious:

1. New developments are expensive, particularly those that have a high technical risk. A rough measure of the technical risk is the amount of engineering effort estimated for that item.

2. Tight schedules are more expensive than a relaxed pace, though too leisurely a schedule is also costly.

Table 9-1
DISCOUNTED COSTS AND SAVINGS PROVIDE PRESENT VALUE ANALYSIS

Year	1	2	3	4	5	6	7	8
Expenditure	1.18	1.18	1.18	1.18	1.18			
Saving	.15	.30	.45	.60	.75	.75	.75	.75
Total	-1.03	-.88	-.73	-.58	-.43	.75	.75	.75
Discounted	-.93	-.72	-.55	-.39	-.26	.42	.38	.35
Present Value	-.93	-1.66	-2.20	-2.60	-2.86	-2.44	-2.05	-1.70

Year	9	10	11	12	13	14	15
Expenditure							
Saving	.75	.75	.75	.75	.75	.75	.75
Total	.75	.75	.75	.75	.75	.75	.75
Discounted	.32	.29	.26	.24	.22	.20	.18
Present Value	-1.38	-1.09	-.83	-.59	-.38	-.18	0.0

3. Manpower requirements during the O&S phase are cost generators because they continue throughout the life of the program. Anything that increases such manpower requirements should be regarded as a cost driver.

4. Any requirement that increases the total force needed to meet the user's specifications is a cost driver. For a weapon, a low kill probability increases the number of weapons needed to cope with a given number of targets.

A list should be developed of the top ten or twenty cost drivers of a system. The above rules may suggest a few candidates. An inverse price list, ranking the purchased parts by price, may suggest other candidates; in production, material costs are much larger than labor costs and warrant close attention. A similar list of the departments that are budgeted with the highest amounts may provide clues for other cost drivers. Each of the functional requirements of the system specification might be ranked in order of cost impact in order to suggest other candidates for the top ten cost drivers.

The cost analyst should compile and publish such a list of cost drivers. The responsible organizations will quickly help the analyst refine the list by claiming that they are certainly not responsible for a cost driver.

As the program progresses and the configuration is defined at more detailed levels, the cost driver list can be defined at correspondingly lower levels. Broad requirements can be eliminated in favor of more detailed constraints. Specific parts should be named rather than subsystems.

The purpose of a similar notion—cost leverage—is to investigate the investment required to eliminate a potential cost. For example, if $10,000 is required in R&D to eliminate $100,000 of support costs, or if $25,000 of manufacturing costs are required to eliminate the same $100,000 of support costs, the better approach is clear.

Note that cost drivers are peculiar to a particular system or class of systems. A continuously operating radar system, for example, will have during its lifetime far higher operating

Table 9-2

MAJOR COST DRIVERS

1.	Preconceived design restrictions	e. g., crew size, number of engines, dimensions
2.	Basing concept	e. g., quantity per base, base location
3.	Operational crew	i. e., quantity, skill types, cross-training, supervision
4.	Billeting	i. e., location
5.	Overhead items	i. e., total labor support costs
6.	Training	e. g., degree of cross-training, proficiency requirements
7.	Training facilities	e. g., location, quantities
8.	Downtime	e. g., reliability requirements, spares requirements

Table 9-2. Major Cost Drivers (Continued)

9. Supply, stockage levels	i.e., percent of confidence or back order level, transportation costs
10. Level of repair	e.g., ease of repair, quantities and types of repair facilities, maintenance personnel
11. Non-reparable concept	i.e., equipment modularization, support equipment
12. Manpower	i.e., skills, turn-over rate, dedication, training
13. Repair facilities	i.e., location, number
14. Contractor involvement	i.e., alternate support concepts
15. Design concept	i.e., the total design

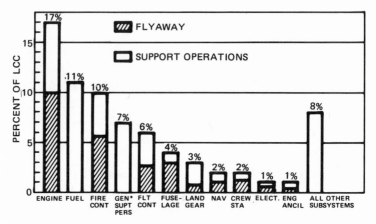

*SERVICING, GROUND HANDLING, SCHEDULED MAINTENANCE, ETC.

Figure 9-8. Systems Have Been Ranked
According to Cost

costs than the sum of its development and procurement costs. Conversely, a missile stored dormant in an ammunition bunker generates few costs, and its development and procurement costs will exceed the operating costs. Therefore, for the radar, operating and support costs will be the predominant cost drivers; for the missile, development and production costs will predominate.

A bar chart of a cost driver list for a military fighter aircraft (Figure 9-8) shows the cost of various subsystems as a proportion of the total LCC. A somewhat different list of cost drivers (Table 9-2) was based on material developed by the National Security Industrial Association's Logistics Management Advisory Committee. Note that the table provides a view different from that of Figure 9-8, emphasizing logistics considerations rather than performance. Common underlying factors on both lists are reliability and maintainability. In preparing a list of cost drivers for a particular program, these two characteristics deserve particular attention.

Design and Design Goals

Design is the central function of the development process, and system engineering and LCC are intended to enhance the design. Goals should be set for the designers of each of the cost elements of LCC that are design-controllable. As discussed earlier, these are first set by an allocation process, starting from the top value, the "affordable cost." This top down process should be taken down to the lowest defined level of the configuration. After these goals are set and published, a bottom up estimate or prediction should be made for each cost element. The variance between the allocation and the prediction is the basis for a reallocation or a redesign or both. Close collaboration between designers and cost analysts is necessary. This is a continuous, ongoing process calling for management skill and determination to prevent cost growth and yet meet the user's needs.

The designer can be assigned the responsibility of meeting the production cost goal (or, at least, the hardware part of production costs, as discussed under *design to cost*); he can also be partially responsible for provisioning costs, support equipment costs, and training costs. The designer may be held responsible for the *number* of operating and maintenance personnel, but do not expect him to know the annual cost of various individuals or supplies; the logistician should be assigned this task. In general, the LCC analyst should endeavor to assign the responsibility for estimating and controlling each cost element to someone other than himself. All of these assignees then become active participants in the LCC process.

Reliability Design

Because improved reliability tends to decrease costs, as shown in Figure 9-9, and because reliability is a design char-

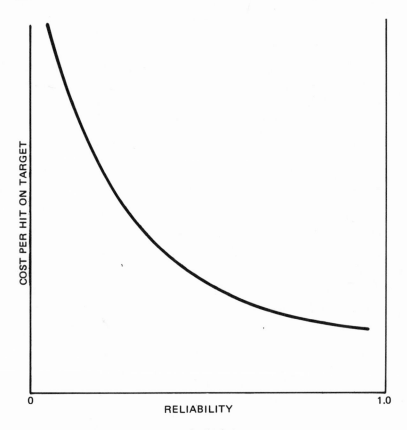

Figure 9-9. Reliability Improvement
Reduces Effective Cost

acteristic, the development process must emphasize reliability. Reliability control methods, such as simplification,
better parts, better analysis, more testing, and redundancy,
must be considered by the designer in the light of their cost
impact.

The designer determines reliability and can change it.
Reliability can be measured and controlled.[3] Note first that
reliability change methods are much better known for electronic and electromechanical devices than for mechanical
devices. The reverse is true for maintainability, where
mechanical devices are well understood, but electronic equip-

ment improvement methods are weaker.[4]

The LCC analyst should understand the basic principles of reliability engineering:

1. The failure rate of an assembly is equal to the sum of the failure rates of its parts.

2. The reliability (probability of no failure) is proportional to the reciprocal of the product of the failure rate and the operating time:

$$R = e^{-(FR)(T)}$$

or approximately

$$R = 1 - (FR)(T) \text{ if } (FR)(T) < .2$$

where

$R =$ Reliability

$FR =$ Failure rate

$T =$ Time

$e =$ Base of the natural logarithms

3. When an approximate parts list is available, a quantitative evaluation of reliability can be made.

The question then is: how much will it cost to change the reliability of a product, and how much reliability change will a dollar buy?[5] Reliability improvements are difficult to achieve, hard to measure, and expensive. Continuously operating equipments can be tested for reliability by laboratory or field tests in a relatively straightforward manner. The sample size and the operating time can be varied to obtain the desired measurement accuracy within the schedule constraints. For products such as missiles, which can be operated only once, the problem is more difficult. Measuring the flight reliability of a missile to an accuracy of, say, 2 percent requires the flight (and expenditure) of at least fifty missiles (by simple arithmetic); statisticians may ask for as many as 200 tests to assure an accuracy of 2 percent. Most reliability improvements considered promise a change of no more than 2 percent. Over and above the cost of designing and installing the change is the cost of determining whether the desired improvement has been achieved. It is thus often necessary to forgo the measurement of the change on the grounds that the beneficial result is intuitively obvious or that laboratory tests indicate a favorable result. The worth of a proposed change may never be demonstrated in the field.

Reliability Change Methods

A number of methods can be used to improve reliability. After systematically evaluating each change method for its reliability impact and its costs, the best method(s) can be selected on the basis of the maximum benefit for the expenditure. Note that the costs of changes should be categorized as either nonrecurring (primarily development and tooling) or recurring (production costs).

Simplification. The best way to improve reliability is to simplify the design. This also reduces production costs. Some of the earliest literature on the subject, which arose out of Samuel Colt's revolver patent case in 1851,[6] explained that the design for a new revolver had fewer parts (was simpler) than existing models and was therefore less likely to fail (more reliable). The cost of such simplification is clearly assignable to design during the R&D phase and is nonrecurring. Because production savings may repay R&D costs, simplification of design may not incur any additional costs and may even provide savings. If so, this is the best of all possible worlds, because reliability improves at no cost. Unfortunately, designers often maintain that the present design is the simplest possible and that further simplification would result in an unacceptable decline in performance. Investment in design investigation for improved reliability may or may not disclose profitable improvements. Even worse, a proposed simplification may make the item more difficult to manufacture and repair, which would raise the LCC. Clearly, the proposed changes must be considered by specialists, such as the production engineer and the maintainability engineer.

It may be possible to get designers to estimate the cost of simplification by asking them to respond to a statement such as, "With one week's work, the design may be simplified by 10 percent, and with a month's work, by 20 percent." Many people would rather comment on such a statement than originate one. For estimating purposes, a 10 percent simplification may be translated into a 10 percent reduction in failure rate (based on a linear relation to complexity). If a more precise conversion is required, the reliability specialist can interpret. The original estimate may not warrant such precision, however.

Better parts. Reliability estimates are usually based on the parts used in the item and their expected failure rates— the lower the expected failure rate, the higher the estimate of reliability. Over the years, much effort has gone into providing better parts, particularly electronic parts. A whole family of military specifications, such as MIL-M-38510, has been written, and parts are available at various levels of reliability assurance, at appropriately elevated costs.[7] These provide an analytically convenient method of deriving a relationship between production cost and reliability. Apparently, the only necessary assumption is that the item's reliability will vary as a function (usually the product) of the individual part reliabilities; that is, the failure rate of the item is the sum of the failure rates of the parts that make it up. This is generally true. The hidden implicit assumption that the use of improved parts is the most economical way to improve reliability is often mistaken, however. Simplification of design, when possible, will have more impact on reliability at a lower cost. The other methods of improving reliability discussed below may be better. In any case, the cost of improving reliability by using better parts is primarily a recurring production cost. The increased costs may be estimated by finding out what specification will be used and getting a purchasing estimate for the desired quantities (the reliability requirements cause high, fixed test costs, independent of quantities).

Better analysis. Many failures during use occur because of an unforeseen combination of circumstances. More complete analysis of the design would allow provisions to preclude such failures. Temperature transients during turn-on and turn-off of electronic equipments cause aging and failures; miniaturized equipment has decreased thermal mass available to cushion transients, and the detrimental effects of temperature cycling are increased. Thorough thermal analyses would disclose such potential problems and allow their prevention. Structural load analysis can similarly preclude mechanical failures. Combined thermal and structural transient load analysis (particularly for aircraft, missiles, and spacecraft) requires elaborate calculations based on a great deal of expensive laboratory and field test data. These tests and analyses are nonrecurring costs during the R&D phase. Some of the analyses will result in changes that increase production costs; usually these production changes cost less than the analysis. The discussion of the cost estimation of analysis and test programs of Chapter 2 is applicable here. If a bottom up method of estimation is used, the working-level estimators provide analogous programs, with the differences for the new task; this provides the basis for reasonableness checks.

Quantitative evaluation of the reliability impact must be done by the designer/analyst who does the job of improved analysis. He can evaluate the failures that the analysis prevented and can estimate the cost of the analysis.

More testing. A widely used model of reliability improve-

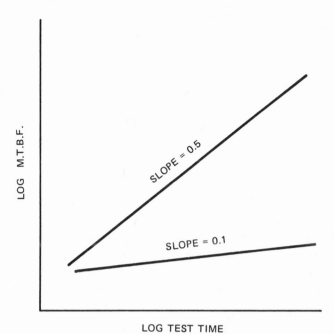

Figure 9-10. Duane Model of Reliability Growth

ment (the Duane model) holds that any change in reliability is a function of the cumulative amount of testing of the equipment. As shown in Figure 9-10, the cumulative test time (both laboratory and field) plotted against the cumulative mean time between failures on log-log graph paper is a straight line. The slope of that line can vary from 0.1 to 0.5. If there is no organized reliability program, the testing provides only the lowest rate of reliability growth (slope 0.1); with a vigorous reliability improvement program, enforced by management, testing produces the highest rate of growth of reliability (slope 0.5). This model has been verified in a large number of programs and is very useful.

To apply the model to an LCC estimate, it is necessary to estimate the value of the slope. Remember that the limits on the slope are really from 0.1 to 0.5; no known programs fall outside these limits. Unless a very convincing case can be made of a truly complete, aggressive reliability program, the slope should be less than 0.4. Average programs justify estimating slopes of 0.2 to 0.3. These reliability program improvements include the previous efforts of simplification, analysis, and better parts; these efforts should *not* be added to the Duane model results. The notion is that test results cause other supplementary efforts.

The cost of additional test time is fairly straightforward; the man-hours required for each hour of test time can be evaluated easily by engineering estimators. The additional cost of the resultant ancillary efforts must also be evaluated. The test program uncovers problems that must be solved; predicting their number and complexity requires experienced judgment. Again the estimating process of analogy, CERs, or grass roots estimates should be followed. Bear in mind that the difficulty of a particular problem for the particular organization can modify the estimate. If the organization has done similar tasks before, the estimate should be conservative. If the design is novel to the organization, provide a more generous manpower estimate; it may be increased by a factor of two. If no one has had a design like this before (advancing the state of the art), the basic problem-solving task may be increased by a factor of three or four.

Production testing can improve field reliability and decrease production costs. Such testing is not subject to the Duane model. Each production item (rather than only qualification test articles) is subjected to environmental (vibration, temperature, shock, or humidity) tests to separate out faulty items. The intensity of the tests must be sufficient to detect problems, but not so great as to create latent defects that the user will later discover in the field. In general, though expensive, production environmental testing has proven to be beneficial; such testing is often used when a proper developmental program is impossible. If feasible, the design department should use the results of the production test to make improvements. Such changes would result in the improvement of the design as predicted by the Duane model. Cost estimation for production environmental tests resembles that for other production activities.

Redundancy. A common method of improving reliability is to provide more than one of a needed item—ranging from an extra piece part to a complete spare system. A great deal of reliability analysis uses redundancy because it is mathematically tractable and the calculation is straightforward and involves no uncertainties. Spares can be "hot" (power on, part of the working system) or "cold" (not activated, either built-in or in a spares cabinet). Hot redundant components can be connected in parallel so that immediate load sharing will follow any failure; alternatively, the spares may require a decision capability to detect the failed component and activate a switching device.

Redundancy is highly cost-effective when one component of the system is markedly less reliable than the others. If that component is also cheap, redundancy is especially recommended. A quantitative cost-benefit analysis can show the advantage of redundancy compared with other reliability change methods. Examine carefully the reliability analysis, since it may often mistakenly assume that there is no connection between the failures of two or more redundant items; usually there are some common causes for failure of all of the redundant items. For example, the switching device often provided to activate redundant items or the additional connectors required for redundancy may have limited reliability. Further, redundancy can complicate fault detection and isolation procedures. In summary, if the hazards of additional cost, misleading analysis, and complicated fault isolation are avoided, redundancy can be a simple, straightforward method of improving reliability.

Reliability Improvement vs. Cost Change

To obtain the optimum relationship between reliability

improvement and cost change, it is necessary to know the cheapest method of improving reliability at each point in the program. More precisely, the reliability improvement method that costs the least for a given amount of failure rate change will have the most favorable benefit. After that improvement method has been used, the next one selected should have the least cost of those remaining for a given amount of failure rate change. This selection criterion ranks the various improvement methods and yields the optimal (minimum) incremental cost for any desired change in reliability.

As an example, let us consider a hypothetical shipboard electronic equipment. The present MTBF is 500 hours. A quantity of 500 is to be produced at a production cost of $50,000 each. Table 9-3 shows the results of a step-by-step estimate of the costs and reliability benefit of each method of improvement. With these results we would first choose the eight man-months of design simplification. Then, an investment in thermal analysis is best. More testing would then be done. If a larger change in reliability were required, the structural analysis might be done, though the testing may have already eliminated some of these problems. The better parts and the redundancy options seem to be far behind. A curve of these results is shown in Figure 9-11. Note that the curve constantly decreases in slope, as each successive improvement is selected on this basis. Of course, these results are speculative (and a little contrived) and are for the purpose of demonstrating the method.

Maintainability Design

The maintainability characteristics of a design, set during the development phase, are second only to reliability features in driving costs of the O&S phase. From a cost point of view, failures (reliability) are significant only because they have to be fixed (the purview of maintainability), and that costs money. As is true for reliability, the designer establishes

Table 9-3

RELIABILITY IMPROVEMENT COST ANALYSIS
(All failure rates 1 per million hours)

SIMPLIFICATION

Two man-months to achieve a 10% simplification

Eight man-months to achieve a 20% simplification

Forty man-months to achieve a 30% simplification

Cost Change	Failure Rate Change	Cost/Failure Rate
$ 10,000	200	50
40,000	400	100
200,000	600	333

BETTER PARTS

Part 1 is now F.R. = 5 and costs $5 each;
replace with F.R. = 1 which costs $10 each
(derating).

Part 2 is now F.R. = 3 and costs $6 each;
replace with F.R. - .5 which costs $16 each.

Part 3 is now F.R. = 1 and costs $5 each;
replace with F.R. = .5 which costs $20 each.

Table 9-3. Reliability Improvement
Cost Analysis (Continued)

Cost Change	Failure Rate Change	Cost/Failure Rate
$ 5 x 500	4.0	417
$10 x 500	2.5	2,000
$15 x 500	0.5	15,000

BETTER ANALYSIS

Structural dynamic analysis will cost six man-months and substantially eliminate vibrational failures which are now 5 percent of the failures.

Additional thermal analysis will cost four man-months and eliminate temperature-caused failures which are now 10 percent of the failures.

Cost Change	Failure Rate Change	Cost/Failure Rate
Structural $30,000	100	300
Thermal $20,000	200	100

Table 9-3. Reliability Improvement
Cost Analysis (Continued)

MORE TESTING

Present test plan is for a total of 600 hours to
achieve the MTBF of 500 hours. Each additional
100 hours of testing will cost 2 man-months in
the test labs and 2 man-months in design
($20,000). Assume an improvement slope of
0.3.

Additional Test Time	MTBF	Failure Rate Change	Cost/Failure Rate
100 Hours	523.7	90	222
200 Hours	545.1	165	242
300 Hours	564.7	229	262

REDUNDANCY

One amplifier with a F.R. 500 costs $2,000 each;
a redundant amplifier would reduce the failure
rate to essentially zero at an additional cost of
$1,500 per assembly.

Cost Change	Failure Rate Change	Cost/Failure Rate
$750,000	500	1,500

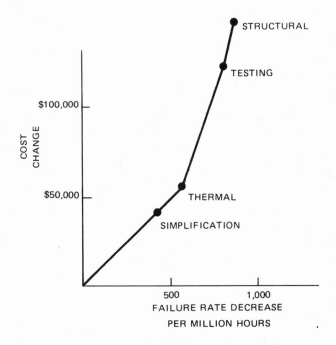

Figure 9-11.   Cost Change for a Change
in Failure Rate

maintainability and can change it. Maintainability can be measured and controlled. The LCC analyst should understand the approach of the maintainability engineer:

1. All maintenance is divided between preventive maintenance (scheduled) and repair (unscheduled). The purpose of preventive maintenance is to decrease the failure rate or to increase equipment life.

2. Repair time is the sum of the preparation time: getting maintenance personnel to the equipment (with tools, test equipments, parts, and instructions), gaining access to the equipment, detecting and isolating the faulty item, removing and replacing the faulty item, checking out renewed operation, and closing up the equipment (assume that the operator detected the fault).

3. The time required for maintenance actions can be calculated as the sum of the times required for elemental tasks

(available in tables).[8]

Maintenance costs include most of the manpower required to support a system, as well as the trucks, test equipment, tools, and so on that constitute the logistics "tail" of a military system. In order to increase the ratio of "teeth" to tail of a weapon, maintainability must be improved. Similar logic applies to other products, from washing machines to automobiles; support costs during the many years of ownership must be controlled. Maintainability engineering provides a number of techniques to do this. Each must be evaluated on the basis of its cost and benefit.

Simplification and Standardization

As in reliability, these are the cheapest methods of improvement, with the most benefits to the maintenance man. The cost of the designer's and the maintainability engineer's creativity and ingenuity is small if done early and does not recur; simplification and standardization may even decrease production costs.

Accessibility and Fault Isolation Provisions

If the replaceable parts are easily accessible, maintenance costs decrease. Improved accessibility costs little during the initial design and rarely increases production costs significantly. The provision of simple methods to detect and isolate faults is really a form of accessibility (functional rather than physical).

The design cost of fault isolation provisions does not recur. Some small production cost increment may be required for an extra tee in the plumbing or an electrical test point, but, again, the production costs are almost negligible. In fact, the reduced cost of fault isolation of production problems may more than offset the increased production costs of additional items.

Test Equipment

Proper test equipment, either built-in or separate, and portable, can also reduce maintenance costs. Automatic, computer-controlled test equipment has become fashionable for more complex systems from automobiles to missiles. The design and acquisition costs of such automatic equipment are large—perhaps 10 to 20 percent of the prime equipment design and acquisition costs. Such test equipment reduces maintenance costs by reducing repair time and personnel skill level requirements.

From the cost standpoint, some qualifications about the use of built-in test equipment are worth considering. First, built-in test equipment must not increase the failure rate of the basic system. If it does, the added maintenance problems may invalidate the original purpose of the test equipment. Second, faulty diagnoses of two kinds are dangerous: if the test equipment condemns good equipment, unnecessary repairs are made; if the test equipment accepts bad equipment, the reliability stays low. These two problems can be compounded if the test equipment blames the failure on the wrong item.

Test equipment should be as extensive and as automatic as possible. Because built-in test equipment has been tailored to the particular item and is immediately available, it is simple and fast to operate. On the other hand, separate portable test equipment, which may already be in the user's inventory, can be used for a number of equipments. Thus, both types of test equipment have features that can reduce costs. Usually, cost trade-offs show that the increased acquisition costs of built-in test equipment are not offset by reduced maintenance costs; built-in test equipment must then be justified, if at all, on the basis of the improved availability of the item.

Maintenance Engineering Analysis

The maintenance engineering analysis (MEA), as discussed

in Chapter 4, formally structures the forgoing efforts by requiring: (1) the discovery and listing of all the logistic resources required to maintain the system; and (2) the minimization of required logistic resources. A somewhat expanded and related method of logistic support analysis (LSA) includes, in addition, all support requirements, such as fuel and ammunition supply operators.[9]

The estimated costs of doing an MEA or LSA should not duplicate the costs of the preceding maintainability improvement tasks, as double accounting would occur. As noted above, the MEA and LSA costs are mainly nonrecurring, with small resultant production costs. Experienced personnel need about two man-days for each page of an MEA.

Maintainability Improvement vs. Cost Change

Improvements in maintainability, in contrast to those in reliability, are fairly easily converted to O&S cost savings. The ratio of the cost of each proposed maintainability task to its anticipated saving in O&S should be calculated. The cost ratio determines the ranking of the proposed maintainability tasks. Table 9-4, an example of a maintainability improvement study, again uses the shipboard equipment example, with an MTTR of 1.5 hours and a ten-year deployment. The results suggest that first priority should go to the eight-manmonth task to simplify, standardize, and improve accessibility, and second priority to the test equipment improvement. If cost is a more important criterion for selection than availability, the fault isolation provisions would not be implemented.

Safety

The military services have recently begun to require that contractors provide system safety programs on large weapon

Table 9-4
MAINTAINABILITY IMPROVEMENTS
COST ANALYSIS

SIMPLIFY, STANDARDIZE AND MORE
ACCESSIBILITY

2 man-months to achieve a 10% reduction in MTTR
and a $10 per unit production cost reduction

8 man-months to achieve a 20% reduction in MTTR
and a $20 per unit production cost reduction

40 man-months to achieve a 30% reduction in MTTR
and a $20 per unit production cost reduction

Cost Change	O&S Cost Change**	Ratio
$ 5,000	$ 39,420	7.9
$ 30,000	$ 78,840	2.6
$190,000	$118,260	0.6

**Repair = (MTTR) (Number of men) (Cost per man-
hour) (Failure rate) (Duty Cycle) (Number of years)
(Hours per year) (Number of equipments).

Table 9-4. Maintainability Improvements
Cost Analysis (Continued)

FAULT ISOLATION PROVISIONS

1 man-month for a 4% reduction in MTTR and a
$50 production cost

3 man-months for an 8% reduction in MTTR and a
$200 production cost

12 man-months for a 12% reduction in MTTR and a
$1,000 production cost

Cost Change	O&S Cost Change	Ratio
$ 30,000	$15,768	.53
$115,000	$31,536	.27
$560,000	$47,304	.08

TEST EQUIPMENT

2 man-months and $100,000 for test equipment
for a 10% reduction in MTTR and a 10% reduction
in scheduled maintenance

6 man-months and $300,000 for test equipment
for a 20% reduction in MTTR and a 20% reduction
in scheduled maintenance

Table 9-4. Maintainability Improvements
Cost Analysis (Continued)

---

24 man-months and $1,000,000 for test equip-
ment for a 30% reduction in MTTR and a 30%
reduction in scheduled maintenance.

Cost Change   O&S Cost Change**   Ratio

$ 110,000 $ 39,420 + $180,000 = $219,420 2.0

$ 330,000 $ 78,840 + $360,000 = $438,840 1.3

$1,120,000 $118,260 + $540,000 = $658,260 0.6

**Repair as before + (Frequency of maintenance)
(Number of Years) (Change in maintenance time)
(Number of men) (Cost per man-hour) (Number
of equipments)

Number of men = 2

Cost per man-hour = $15

Duty Cycle = .1

Frequency of scheduled maintenance = 12
per year.

system development, just as civil authorities now do for such major installations as nuclear power plants, petroleum refineries, and dams, or as the Occupational Safety and Health Act does for consumer products. The cost of the required safety engineering has therefore increased and is part of the R&D cost estimate. LCC estimates have usually not incorporated the cost of accidents, both because it is hard to place a money value on the loss of life, injuries, schedule delays, and loss of prestige and public esteem, and because the probabilistic nature of accidents makes them difficult to handle in an accounting sense.

In the past, the LCC estimate included only a qualitative statement on safety, or safety hazards, leaving it to the decision maker to evaluate the total ownership cost of the system. Safety statements generally fit into one of the following four categories:

1. the claim that the equipment poses no significant safety hazards
2. the statement that the equipment poses no safety hazards to external areas, accompanied by a list of possible accidents and their consequences to the equipment
3. the claim that the item poses no safety hazards to the public
4. a list of the safety hazards to external areas, accompanied by an account of the efforts made to contain them

Recent studies of dams[10] and aircraft[11] show that quantitative evaluation of the cost of disasters is possible and significant. They state that the cost of a hazard can be found by evaluating its probability and the cost of the potential disaster. The product of the probability and the cost is the "expected value" of the hazard and should be part of the LCC estimate. For example, the expected value of a dam failure with a probability as small as 1 in 10,000 dam-years is more than a quarter of the dam's total LCC.

Design to Cost

Design selection during development largely determines production cost. Recognizing this, the DOD has directed that production costs be controlled during design.[12] Such control of design is important not only because production costs are a large part of LCC, but also because it is difficult to control LCC by contractual methods. The DOD has used production cost as a surrogate for LCC. At the same time, DOD directives insist that production cost goals must not be achieved at the expense of LCC goals. Management effort to control production costs during design is the design to cost (DTC) program. Such design cost control efforts are common to both commercial and military practice; a similar, older effort that started in commercial practice is called value engineering.

The DTC effort involves goal setting; cost reduction methods used during design; estimating methods; procedures for tracking, controlling, and reporting costs; vendor and subcontractor integration into the prime contractor's effort; and the solution of various DTC problems.

Successful design cost control programs establish a cost goal at the beginning of the program.[13] The DTC goal includes the nonrecurring production costs (e.g., tooling, manufacturing planning, test equipment) and the recurring costs of unit production (i.e., direct labor, overhead, material, and subcontract costs) as shown in Figure 9-12. Because the designer controls only the recurring costs (overhead is in direct proportion to labor and material costs), he can be made responsible for them. The resultant designer-oriented effort is labeled "design to unit production cost" (DTUPC). Cost becomes as much of a factor in design as weight or power consumption. A DTUPC program has these elements:

1. a goal-setting procedure, dividing the top cost goal among subordinate parts

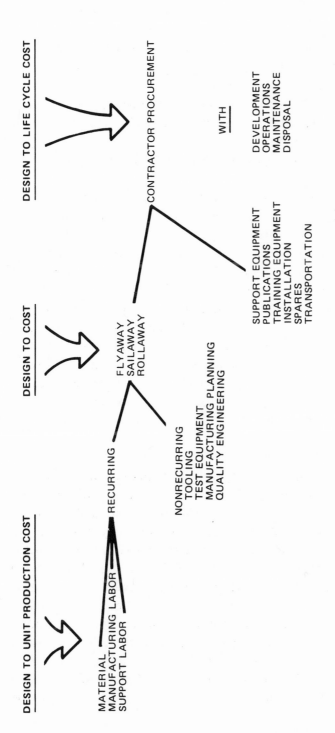

Figure 9-12. Design to Unit Production Cost
is the designer-controllable part of design to cost

2. design guidelines with possible production methods to reduce costs; cost reviews or workshops to assist designers
3. a cost-estimating method for each level of design with a method of capturing the design characteristics during the design process
4. a procedure to track, control, and report unit production cost
5. the integration of subcontractors and vendors into the program, just as if they were part of the in-house engineering effort
6. integration of the DTUPC program with the LCC effort

Care should be taken that the DTUPC emphasis on unit production cost does not deemphasize the cost of tools and test equipment and the impact of production rate and quantity on these. Clearly, production methods and tools (the nonrecurring cost determinants) will change as the production rate and quantity change. The design of an item should therefore change as the planning for production changes.

Goal Setting

The top cost goal established by the system engineering effort is often ·incorporated into the contract with the customer. System engineers (or design to cost specialists) should set the goal carefully, because too low a goal will be dismissed by the designers as naive and hopeless and too high a goal achieves nothing but ridicule. They should define the content of the cost goal precisely and assure that all of its elements are controllable by the contractor; an external, uncontrollable cost element decreases designer motivation. Occasionally, the cost goal for the entire product is broken down by one level of the WBS in the contract and is subsequently monitored at that level by the customer. The contractor must allocate the cost goal, or goals, down the

"DESIGN TO" REQUIREMENTS SUMMARY WORKSHEET FOR DESIGN TO COST

PROJECT _____ DESIGNER _____

ASSEMBLY _____ DATE _____

NEXT ASSEMBLY _____ REVISION _____

SCHEDULE "DESIGN TO" REQUIREMENTS STATE

ON _____ IS _____ %

NOTES

DESIGN TO REQUIREMENTS	SOURCE (SPECIFY ORGANIZATION AND PERSON)	SOURCE DOCUMENT IDENTIFICATION	NOTE NO	DATE OF LAST REVISION	STATE IN %
1 DEFINITION (WHAT IS IT?)					
2 PERFORMANCE AND FUNCTIONS					
3 PHYSICAL INTERFACE					
4 ELECTRICAL INTERFACE					
5 ENVELOPE					
6 WEIGHT					
7 EMC (EMISSION AND SUSCEPTIBILITY)					
8 CLIMATIC (TEMP, HUMIDITY, ETC)					
9 STRUCTURAL (SHOCK VIBRATION, ETC)					
10 COST (PROD UNIT COST AND PROD QTY)					
11 TEST AND DUTY CYCLE					
12 REQUIRED MIL SPECS AND STANDARDS					
13 RELIABILITY AND SAFETY MARGIN					
14 MAINTAINABILITY AND INTERCHANGEABILITY					
15 PRODUCIBILITY (STD PARTS AND YIELD)					
16 OTHER (DESCRIBE)					

Figure 9-13. Worksheet for Design To Cost

WBS to a level at which individual designers can be held responsible. This allocation process must involve the designers, and they must agree that the resultant goals are challenging but achievable. During the design process, goals are regarded as fixed; if change is imperative, any increase in one goal should be matched by a corresponding decrease in another goal.

This assumes a clear design concept and requirements at the time of goal setting. If the concept and requirements change in the course of the development, the pressures for change in cost goals may be irresistible.

Cost-Reduction Methods during Design

The task of cost reduction in design essentially requires identification of the major cost elements, such as the LCC drivers, and methods to eliminate or minimize their cost.[14] Trade-off studies, as discussed earlier in this chapter for LCC,

SERIAL NO. ______

DESIGN SELECTION NOTICE (DSN) SHEET ____ OF ____

ITEM ________________ DATE ________________

N/A ________________ DESIGNER ________________

PROGRAM ________ DTC PHASE ________ SECTION ________________

DESIGN TO REQUIREMENTS

DOCUMENTS: KEY PARAMETERS:

COST TARGET (PRODUCTION UNIT) IS $________

DESIGN ALTERNATIVES AND ASSESSMENTS

DESIGN SELECTION

DESCRIPTION, RATIONALE & LIMITATIONS:

PRODUCTION UNIT COST STATUS

ESTIMATED COST OF
SELECTED DESIGN APPROACH IS $________
FOR 19__ DOLLARS. PROD. QUANT ______

PME ________________ DATE

PYA ________________ DATE

DESIGNER	DATE	SECTION HEAD	DATE	CENTER MANAGER	DATE

Figure 9-14. Design Selection Notice (DSN)

are also done for DTUPC. An ordered, structured approach to cost reduction is necessary, with the requirements documented, as in Figure 9-13, and the alternatives defined, as in Figure 9-14. DTUPC workshops, with various specialists assisting, can aid the designer.

A key problem is identifying the *real* cost drivers and their cause. Is the cost driver the large amount of machining that must be done, or the product accuracy requirement that necessitates the machining? Can the accuracy requirement be relaxed or achieved differently so that the machining can be eliminated? Is all the machining necessary? Are the tolerances really required, or are the figures just customary? Can a standard part, already designed and in production, be used or adapted?

The use of available designs minimizes the estimating task in addition to reducing costs. Designers should be dissuaded or cajoled away from the "not invented here" syndrome that denigrates the designs of others. They may then have more time to perfect an elegant design that does have to be "invented here."

In essence, DTUPC and DTC mean that cost and performance are equally important design constraints. The designer can trade performance for cost. He can be sensitive to the critical areas where small changes in performance requirements cause large changes in cost; the performance requirements can be modified to avoid the cost increase. Perceptive managers will encourage worthwhile changes in such areas and will protect only the essential performance thresholds.

The scheduling of cost trade-offs can determine their effectiveness. If the trade-offs occur too early, there is not enough information to make intelligent decisions. Later, high sunk costs can discourage changes, with the result that decisions tend to become self-justifying.

Estimating Methods

The estimating methods used for DTUPC and DTC are those discussed in Chapter 3. To be useful for the design process, the estimating methods must be adapted to serve the designer promptly and easily. The designer must either have the information to do the estimates himself or be able to get such estimates from the specialists. Conferences with such cost-estimating specialists at the layout or schematic stage of the design are invaluable. A sample estimating form (Figure

WBS: _____   DATE: _____

CPC #: _____

DESCRIPTION: _____   OTHER: _____

ELEMENT	HOURS	COST	RATE	TOTAL COST
MATERIAL				
BASIC MATERIAL (CODE 2-3)				
RAW MATERIAL				
AMC				
SUB-TOTAL				
TEST				
SUB-TOTAL				
CODE 1				
TOTAL				
TAXES & INSURANCE				
TOTAL COST				
PROFIT				
PRICE				
DIRECT LABOR				
MANUFACTURING				
MANUFACTURING INSPECTION				
PROCUREMENT INSPECTION				
TOTAL DIRECT LABOR				
OVERHEAD				
OTHER COSTS				
PROCUREMENT INSPECTION, T & P/D				
OTHERS				
GENERAL & ADMINISTRATIVE EXPENSE				
TAXES & INSURANCE				
SUB-TOTAL COST				
TOTAL COST				
PROFIT				
PRICE				
COST OF MONEY				
TBRC PRICE				
TOTAL PRICE				

Figure 9-15. Manufacturing Estimating Form

9-15) is useful for manufacturing costs. A computerized estimating system, such as the RCA PRICE model, can give the designer easy access to cost estimates. Keep in mind the necessity for knowledgeable use of such computer programs, as recommended in Chapter 3.

Tracking, Controlling, and Reporting Procedures

A tracking, controlling, and reporting procedure for the

costs of the design helps to assure the achievement of cost goals. This procedure is part of the technical performance measurement system discussed above. A large organization would be wise to use a DTUPC model for this function and a computer to store and print out the data. The model is essentially the WBS, with some method of adding the costs at each hierarchical level. This model describes the design at each stage of its progress. The computer compares the most recent reports of estimated costs with the goals at each level of the WBS. A report shows the deviations from the goals and names the responsible designer and design organization. A progress report with a graph gives the status of the total program and of major subsystems.

The Stinger guided missile DTUPC results (Figure 9-16) are particularly interesting because they show the result of management intervention. When the cost estimates started to exceed the affordable goals, both customer and contractor management took decisive action to reverse the growth in costs. The complete control and review process calls for management involvement and approval from both sides. The customer, in particular, assures that the only acceptable basis for increasing the overall cost goal is a decrease in LCC; conversely, design cost goal improvements are not to be made at a sacrifice in LCC.

The use of a computerized control method provides a means of accumulating a cost data bank for future projects. A measure of variability or risk derived from the history of a cost estimate can assist in future selections among various program alternatives.

Vendors and Subcontractor Integration

Most systems under DTC and DTUPC programs include substantial amounts (usually more than half) of subcontracted and purchased material costs. These should be included in the design cost control program. The subcon-

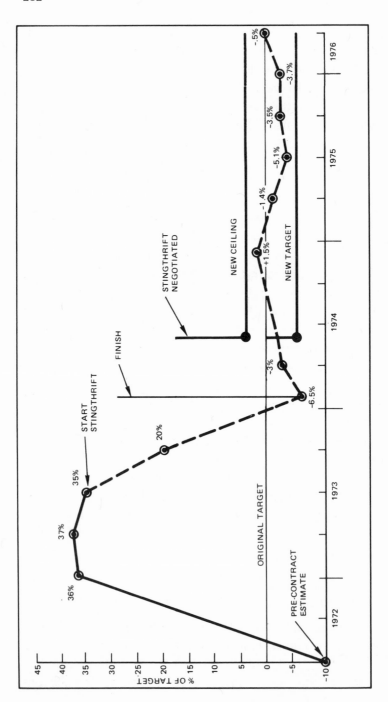

Figure 9–16. Design–to–Cost Progress vs. Time

tractors who have a design responsibility should be treated like one of the prime contractor's design groups; the subcontractor should participate in the setting of cost goals; he should be assigned goals, should be required to report periodically on progress toward these goals, and should receive summary reports as issued. Vendors, on the other hand, should be informed of the effort to reduce costs and should be asked to suggest how the selection or application of their products could reduce costs. Of course, vendors regularly attempt to reduce costs for competitive reasons, and their efforts should be encouraged. But they should not be required to conduct cost reduction programs for the prime contractor's item unless the prime contractor finances such efforts; these are usually single purpose items for which the vendor anticipates no additional sales.

DTC Problems

The relationship between DTC or DTUPC and LCC is a difficult contractual problem. Because it has not yet been possible to provide a contractual incentive for the entire LCC, the production cost goals (from DTC or DTUPC) are often the sole cost consideration in design. The contractor tries to decrease production costs, even if LCC suffers. The buyer must increase surveillance over the contractor's activities to prevent this. Other incentive clauses, such as schedule or reliability, cause a similar situation, in that the contractor strives to maximize profits by emphasizing that incentive characteristic to the possible neglect of other characteristics. More balanced or more encompassing incentive schemes would alleviate these situations.

Manufacturing estimating methods are often insensitive to design details. These estimating methods are approximations and envision average designs. Therefore, when a designer does incorporate detail changes for cost reduction, the estimate may not show a change. Even worse, some cost reduction changes may even increase the cost estimate. For example, the addition of a test connector may simplify testing, enhance quality, and assure that the item works before it is incorporated into the next assembly. This effect should increase the yield of the production process. The estimating method uses an average yield rate, however, and only sees that an added connector is an additional cost. Therefore the designer has added a feature that seems to decrease the production cost, but the estimating method foresees an increase in cost. As cost-estimating techniques are refined, perhaps with the assistance of computers, the dilemma should lessen.

The data base for cost control perennially needs enlargement and improvement. There are no systematic methods whereby contractors may exchange cost data. Cost reduction methods and data are only superficially discussed in technical journals and textbooks. Many contractors consider cost data so private that they even impede their own employees' access to such information (a self-defeating tactic). A possible source of cost data is the government, as a buyer; publication of procurement cost data in easily accessible form, conveniently cataloged, would be of major assistance to DTC and DTUPC programs. Unfortunately, the few current compendiums of such data omit vital information on the quantities procured and other conditions of the contract.

Logistics

Logistics planning is an essential part of the system engineering effort because logistics support cannot be economically developed after the product has been designed and delivered to the user. LCC analysis should alert the developer to the cost implications of development decisions for the user. This requires a two-way communication. The user must describe how he intends to use the product and his concept of its maintenance. At what levels will what types of maintenance be carried out? For example, will repairs requiring a soldering iron be made at the organizational level? Will the emergency service truck replace fan belts as well as change tires? Such decisions can affect design concepts. On the other hand, the designer may be able to show that this particular design allows unskilled personnel to change fan belts without danger. The user may not be aware of the cost of some of the policy constraints he has imposed. Note that logistics considerations differ from maintainability. Maintainability is concerned with the design itself—whether it is possible to maintain a particular item. Logistics goes beyond this to a concern with field doctrine; what kind of maintenance facilities to provide at various locations and the levels of personnel skills available.

For logistics problems also, cost trade-offs are helpful. For example, if the reliability requirements are very expensive to implement, it may be cheaper to achieve the required availability with a fast resupply technique. Only a quantitative cost trade-off can provide a definitive answer. As another example, Table 9-5 quantifies the choice between built-in test equipment and separable test equipment. Note the difference in repair times and skill requirements using the different equipments. This limited trade-off considers only some of the factors affecting cost; a broader study would include (1) the cost of the change in the availability of the guns, (2) the cost of using each separable test equipment for more guns at some sacrifice in the repair time, and (3) the possible change in reliability arising from the inherent difference in capability of the two types of test equipment. Even a limited analysis improves on a completely intuitive judgment, so long as the decision maker realizes that some factors still require judgment.

Most users need innovative support concepts. Organizational rigidities tend to prevent the advocacy of new ideas. The developer can often provide such new thoughts because,

Table 9 – 5

BUILT-IN TEST EQUIPMENT VS. SEPARABLE TEST EQUIPMENT
FOR A
RADAR-DIRECTED GUN

Cost Category	Built-in Test Equipment	Separable Test Equipment
R & D	No change	No change
Acquisition	$20,000 per gun	$30,000 for each of 4 guns
Operation and Support: 10 years Maintenance manpower	Repair time 20 minutes 2 men @ $10 per hour 40 failures per year per gun 40 x 2 x 20/60 x 10 x 10 = $2,667 per gun	Repair time 70 minutes 2 men @ $12 per hour 40 failures per year per gun 40 x 2 x 70/60 x 12 x 10 = $11,200 per gun
Total Cost for 4 guns	$80,000 Acquisition $10,667 Maintenance $90,667 Total	$30,000 Acquisition $44,800 Maintenance $74,800 Total

as an outsider, he is unencumbered by preconceived notions and is aware of the new technology available. It may still be difficult, however, to realize potential cost savings in the user environment of fixed habits and jealously guarded prerogatives.

Summary

1. Make LCC part of the system development. Design to life cycle cost.

2. Highlight the cost drivers.

3. Reliability and maintainability determine the largest part of the operating costs. Control over both of them minimizes costs.

4. Provide the decision makers with cost comparisons of alternatives.

5. Work at minimizing LCC at all levels of detail; total LCC thereby decreases even if the entire system cannot be analyzed.

6. Reduce the production cost, but guard against adverse effects on LCC.

Notes

1. U.S. Executive Office of the President, Office of Management and Budget, *Major Systems Acquisition*, Bulletin A 109 (Washington, D.C.: Government Printing Office, April 5, 1976).

2. U.S. Department of Defense, *Engineering Management*, MIL-STD-499A(USAF) (Washington, D.C.: Department of Defense, 1974).

3. Igor Bazovsky, *Reliability Theory and Practice* (Englewood Cliffs, N.J.: Prentice-Hall, 1961).

4. Because of the rapid advance in electronics, this rule may be changing; solid state electronics, in particular, devel-

ops faster than reliability data gathering.

5. The schedule impact of reliability change (usually a delay for more development work) may be translated into money terms or left as a footnote "cost."

6. Martin Rywell, *The Trial of Samuel Colt* (Harriman, Tenn.: Pioneer Press, 1953).

7. U.S. Department of Defense, *General Specification for Microcircuits,* MIL-M-38510 (Washington, D.C.: Department of Defense, 1976).

8. U.S. Department of Defense, *Maintainability Prediction,* MIL-HDBK-472 (Washington, D.C.: Department of Defense, 1966).

9. U.S. Department of Defense, *Logistic Support Analysis,* MIL-STD-1388-1 and -2 (Washington, D.C.: Department of Defense, 1976).

10. R. K. Mark and D. E. Stuart-Alexander, "Disaster as a Necessary Part of Benefit-Cost Analysis," *Science,* September 16, 1977.

11. Kenneth A. Solomon and David Okrent, "Hazard Prevention," *Journal of the System Safety Society,* January-February 1975.

12. U.S. Department of Defense, *Design to Cost,* DOD Directive 5000.28 (Washington, D.C., 1975).

13. Major General Frank A. Hinrichs, "Design to Cost Requires Common Understanding, Clear Direction," *Defense Management Journal,* July 1974; U.S. Air Force, *Handbook for the Implementation of the Design to Cost Concept,* SA-TR-75-2, Directorate of Aerospace Studies, Kirtland Air Force Base, New Mexico, 1975.

14. H. E. Trucks, *Designing for Economical Production* (Dearborn, Mich.: Society of Manufacturing Engineers, 1974), provides a detailed discussion of various high cost elements (such as machine parts) and suggests ways of reducing costs.

10
Management Audit and Control

The user of an LCC estimate must exercise control over the estimating process to insure that valid, dependable results are obtained. Control may be exercised at many levels, from the analyst's immediate supervisor to the highest executive and legislative offices; this includes both buyer and seller management, for the techniques are the same for both. The controls used at each level operate similarly, differing only in the amount of detail required and not at all in kind.

Two basic methods will further management supervision over an LCC estimate: (1) program evaluation: how was the estimating process done? (2) estimate validation: what are the values of the estimate, and how do they compare with other estimates? When a manager is satisfied with the estimate, he must judge whether decisions can be made on the basis of the estimate.

Program Evaluation

Management (contractor and buyer) should periodically evaluate the LCC program (including DTC) for its adequacy. The following checklist, based on presentations by Robert Bidwell, enables the reviewer to ascertain the quality of the estimating:[1]

1. Has a qualified LCC management representative been appointed? Has he the requisite authority and organizational status?

2. Has a cost model been constructed with sufficient detail for control use? Is it sensitive to the planning and design work being done?

3. Have cost drivers been identified for at least 80 percent of the total estimated life cycle (or production) costs?

4. Has special management attention been given to the top ten cost drivers to see whether economies are feasible?

5. Has management defined the relative priority of cost in relation to performance, delivery schedule, and other requirements?

6. Are the planning and design groups aware of the LCC/DTC cost targets for their areas of responsibility?

7. Is the status of each group's cost efforts circulated on a weekly (biweekly or monthly) interval to the groups and their supervision? Are variances visible? Are reports made of actions to correct variances?

8. Is estimating support available to the design groups? How prompt is it?

9. Are the LCC and DTC requirements incorporated into design subcontracts?

10. Are design subcontractors subject to these same program evaluation criteria?

11. Is the cost performance of subcontractors reviewed periodically (at least bimonthly)?

12. Has the buyer been told which of his requirements are the top ten cost drivers? Have ways of reducing such costs been suggested?

13. Can the cost estimates be validated by an independent appraisal?

14. Have all cost estimates been assigned a "level of maturity" or other indication of risk? Are the basis for and soundness of the estimates visible?

15. Are the cost-estimating methods used sound? Are

estimates based on prior experience with similar work? Have learning curves been used properly, based on prior experience?

16. Has a broad data base been gathered for cost estimating?

17. Have inflation and discounting factors been adequately considered?

18. Have trade-off studies been made? Are the results used or applied?

19. Are the DTC and LCC work coordinated? Do DTC decisions include consideration of LCC?

20. Are the reliability, maintainability, and system safety programs compatible with LCC requirements?

21. Has each organization involved in the program been formally informed of its cost goals? Have all responded?

An evaluation of this kind may disclose as many problems for the reviewer as for the organization being reviewed, for it probes management intent and dedication. Of course, the purposes of the LCC effort—such as (1) long-range planning and budgeting, (2) comparing competitive programs, or (3) controlling an ongoing program—influence the depth of work.

Validation of Estimates

To assure an effective LCC effort, management should require periodic presentations of LCC estimates. Such presentations may be oral, with charts and other visual aides, or, preferably, written memorandums for the record. Continuity from review to review is important, because the examination of changes is the most powerful way of validating an estimate. Management can validate the estimate presented by systematically examining the content of the reports, by comparing estimates, and by analyzing trends.

Content of LCC Estimate Reports

Each LCC estimate report should include:

1. A statement explaining assumptions and ground rules (see Table 7-2). Changes from previous assumptions are particularly important.

2. A description of the cost model. The cost elements, how the costs are combined to obtain the total estimate, and the work breakdown structure or other costing structure should be mentioned. Even if they have been discussed in previous reports, the audience needs reminding.

3. An enumeration of the data sources used. The audience must be able to evaluate the basis of the estimate. New or changed data sources deserve particular mention. Comments on the validity of the data sources and comparisons with alternate sources are helpful. The quantitative impact of the change on the total estimate should be shown.

4. A brief statement about the cost-estimating relations (CERs) used and their derivation. LCC analysts know that the CERs are the foundation of the estimate and are the most technically challenging part of the estimate. Sophisticated reviewers should have the opportunity to understand the CERs, their logic, and rationale.

5. The total estimate in dollars (thousands, millions, or billions—the units partially imply accuracy). This total estimate should be divided into the various categories of interest to the particular audience and shown at the level of detail appropriate for that audience. The immediate supervisor of the LCC analyst should examine the lowest level of the work or cost-breakdown structure; the program manager usually goes only to the third level of the structure but scrutinizes trouble areas in finer detail. Executives may need only the breakdown by program phases and by expenditure classes. Last, and most important, the dollar value of the previous LCC estimate should be displayed for comparison. If possible, the comparable chart or figure used in the last

presentation should be shown.

6. The current status of any contractual cost incentives or requirements such as RIW, target logistic support cost, DTC, or others. What is the expected final outcome for each incentive or requirement? What incentive payment is foreseen? Are there any problems requiring remedial action? If so, what is being done, and with what effect?

7. A description of the sensitivity analyses performed and their results. Avoid the common mistake of enveloping sensitivity analyses in technical jargon. Simple, understandable results are welcomed. Show the conclusions.

8. A comparison with other means of estimating the LCC. Such a comparison enhances the reviewer's confidence in the process. Either the estimator or an "independent auditor" (see below) may present the comparison. The best comparisons use programs familiar to the audience and show how this LCC estimate can be derived from the known costs of the familiar program. "Reasonableness checks" are less structured ways of doing this.

9. The conclusions and significance of the estimate. This summary interests the audience most. Statements such as "this is half of next year's budget" or "the cost change is due to the policy change made during the last period" increase the impact of the estimate. Bare numbers often do not impress an audience.

Despite all of the above, brevity is often more important than completeness. The presenter's skill is shown by what is successfully relegated to appendixes.

Comparative Estimates

In conjunction with its own review of periodic LCC estimate reports, management should obtain independent estimates of LCC. The occasional use of independent cost estimates can establish the validity of the in-house process. The second estimate may be done by another in-house group or by an outside contractor or by the customer.

Since there may be no basis for comparing two completely separate estimates, some coordination is necessary; the coordination should be arranged to compromise the independence of the second estimate minimally. For example, the ground rules and assumptions of the first estimate should be made available to the second estimator, for use or modification. Similarly, the data sources for the first estimate should be made available to the second estimator, but with no edict to use them.

An independent auditor usually has more expertise or status or both than the original analyst. For these reasons, the independent is apt to be busier and more expensive, and his estimate is likely to use shortcuts. Such use of a different method enhances the value of the comparison.

The second estimate should present its results in the same format as the basic estimate, or should at least use a similar one. Remember that the audience must be able to compare the two estimates.

Management Review of LCC Estimate Reports

In examining the LCC analyst's presentation, a reviewer should first analyze its statement of ground rules and assumptions to be sure that reviewer and analyst agree that these rules and assumptions apply to the program. Are the assumptions merely for the convenience of the estimator? Do they distort the results? Has the analyst ruled out the difficult tasks? For example, was the effect of inflation ruled out because it has an equal effect on all alternatives, or because it was too onerous to predict? Are the ground rules reasonable? Are they clearly explained? A valid but obscure rule may jeopardize an entire estimate. In a recent competitive estimate, it was stated without justification that the maintenance manpower was three men. That bidder lost the competition on the basis of inadequate understanding of the maintenance problem. In reality, the bidder had a novel maintenance concept that truly lowered the maintenance requirements.

Is the estimate complete? Does it include all of the significant costs correctly? For example, provisioning is often most expensive and inadequately estimated; the estimate is often on a "should cost" basis, failing to recognize what most likely will happen under usual provisioning procedures.

Much of the remaining information on the presentation may be ignored, unless the reviewer wants to check a particular cost value. He should, however, go to the bottom line and compare it with other estimates. Does it make sense? Should this program really cost, say, twice as much as another program? Can it really be compared with that program? Are better comparisons possible? Does another company, another service, another country have a program that compares with some part of this program? As the manager, the reviewer has a broader background than the LCC analyst and should know about more comparable programs. If the analyst complains about his lack of information on other programs, the reviewer should use his broader contacts to provide some help.

Next, the reviewer should examine changes in the LCC estimate. Has the analyst incorporated all changes in the program makeup since the last time? For example, if an operational base has been eliminated in the interim, does the new LCC estimate show the resultant cost change? Was the cost change commensurate with its cause? Is the analyst hiding the correction of any previous mistakes behind the program change? If there are policy changes since the last review, are they reflected in the cost estimates? For example, if it was decided to train all operators in maintenance as well as operation in order to reduce operations and maintenance costs, the effect should be seen in the LCC estimate. If such a policy change had no effect on costs, there is a problem either in the policy decision or in the LCC estimating process.

Trend Analysis

Finally, the reviewer should study how the LCC estimates have varied over time. Some of the cost changes are due to changes in the scope of the program and are valid reasons for the estimate to change. Others are in the nature of predictable problems. The analyst's ability to anticipate the general nature and magnitude of such changes is a good measure of his worth. Such changes are not considered valid excuses for changes in the LCC estimate.

Valid Reasons for Change	*Invalid Reasons for Change*
Quantity of production	Inflation
Schedule	Technical problems
Performance requirements	Subcontractor problems
Contractual clauses, e.g.,	Contractor or customer
DOD patent rights	management problems

Note that these changes in scope must be real changes; a new interpretation of a previous requirement or a firmer definition of a contractual requirement is not a change in scope.

With the effects of the valid changes removed, the reviewer can see the changes caused by the estimating process. Is there a consistent trend toward rising or falling costs? Is the variability about the trend line increasing or decreasing? Some possible patterns are shown in Figure 10-1. The time series analysis of Box and Jenkins mentioned earlier offers a systematic method of forecasting the final value of a series of LCC estimates.[2]

Decision Criteria

When should management take action on the basis of an LCC estimate? For budgeting or program planning purposes, the only decision necessary is whether the estimate as a whole is good enough to use or reject. The review methods discussed above should provide the basis for such acceptance

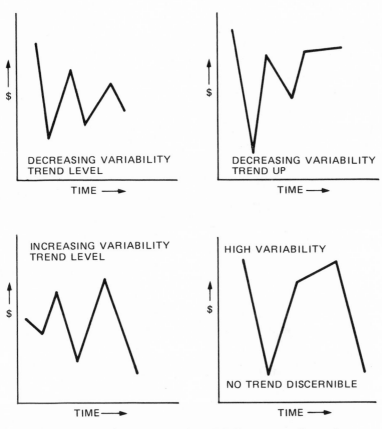

Figure 10-1. Successive LCC Estimates Reveal
Estimating   Ability

or rejection.

In deciding between competing programs, the problem is, "What difference in cost justifies a decision in favor of one program in a competition?" All else being equal, this problem requires an understanding of the precision of comparative estimates. LCC estimates are rarely able to achieve an error of less than 5 percent; this must be regarded as a limit. At the other extreme, comparative estimates are always more accurate than a factor of two. They are more dependable because errors in each of the compared systems tend to be in the same, compensating direction; they also tend to be somewhat *better* than the data sources as the analyst compares a number of data sources and selects the most likely values. If one cost estimate is more than 50 percent higher than the other, therefore, this should be considered significant. Differences as small as 20 percent can be considered significant if the estimates are well grounded and are for conventional programs with good background data. Differences of less than 20 percent should be carefully examined before a decision.

For the control of ongoing programs, changes of very small amounts in LCC estimates should be considered significant. Changes of 1 or 2 percent may indicate problems, because the more recent estimate is based on data and methods that are at least as good as those of the previous estimate.

Summary

1. The LCC effort will be only as good as management makes it.

2. Management must audit the LCC program. A checklist of desirable features of an LCC program should be reviewed regularly.

3. The comparison of two or more "independent" estimates enhances confidence.

4. Program changes should be examined to note the effect on the LCC estimate.

5. All LCC estimate changes should be explained.

6. Differences of 20 percent between competing LCC estimates justify a choice; changes of 2 percent between the last estimate and the current one signify trouble.

Notes

1. Robert L. Bidwell, director, Product Engineering Services Office, Department of Defense, Washington, D.C.

2. Thomas J. Boardman and Maurice C. Bryson, "A Review of Some Smoothing and Forecasting Techniques," *Journal of Quality Technology* 10, no. 1 (January 1978); Vincent A. Mabert, *An Introduction to Short-Term Forecasting Using Box-Jenkins Methodology* (Norcross, Ga.: Production Planning and Control Division, American Institute of Industrial Engineers, 1975). These sources provide a more accessible discussion of time series analysis than the mathematically rigorous treatment of George E. P. Box and Gwilyn M. Jenkins, *Time Series Analysis: Forecasting and Control* (San Francisco: Holden-Day, 1970).

11
Management Strategy

Once the basic techniques have been mastered, the winning strategies must be considered. Both the buyer and the contractor must understand that their mutual long-range objective is to minimize total cost and cost risk. The buyer and the seller will profit from strategies that decrease LCC and its possible variability, because the program will derive the maximum benefit from limited resources.

Judicious users of LCC recognize that it is not the preeminent *desirable characteristic* in the development and use of matériel; it is an important factor to be balanced against three or four other equally important considerations: performance, schedule, immediate costs, and perhaps marketing strategy. No formula is available for such trade-offs. Management must judge the relative importance of each factor and, on that basis, try to enhance each within the constraints caused by each of them. For example, perhaps a six-month-longer production schedule will lower the immediate costs by 10 percent and the LCC estimate by 5 percent; management (both buyer and seller) must decide whether the delay is worth the lowered costs. This decision must evaluate the immediate and the long-range effect of both the delay and the improved costs vis-à-vis other competitive programs (marketing strategy). The service chief and the Congress may differ as to the relative importance of a program that operates on schedule as against one that takes six months longer but provides cost savings; the next Congress may evaluate these factors differently, particularly if there are changes in the availability of money or in the perceived need for the product. The manager's evaluation of such relationships is subjective, not analytical. Discerning management will recognize LCC as one of the important quantifiable program attributes and will seek to take a balanced view.

The government buyer and the contractor can use specific strategies to enhance their relative positions. Although the following comments are separately addressed to buyer and contractor, many apply to both; government procurement agencies usually act as both a buyer from industry and as a seller to the using agency, and so both sets of comments apply to them.

Make LCC Significant

Buyer. The government must convince contract bidders that LCC is a significant consideration in the selection of a contractor and in the continued viability of the program. This must be enunciated clearly by the engineering and planning personnel, as well as by the financial and managerial people. During the source selection process, LCC must have a conspicuous rank in the listing of evaluation criteria. In order to continue to impress the contractor, there must be adequate financial incentives to improve LCC. Moreover, the reward for improving cost performance must be high enough to make the contractor's effort worthwhile. Any legalistic caveats from the procurement organization's experts about the Armed Services Procurement Regulations (ASPR) or similar controls, which purportedly prohibit such incentives, should be challenged. The ASPR do not prohibit incentives that benefit the government; if other controls impede an adequate incentive structure, exceptions can be obtained. Finally, an ongoing review of the LCC estimates, as discussed in Chapter 10, emphasizes the importance of LCC.

Contractor. The contractor must make credible his ability and determination to control and decrease LCC. Several ways to go about this are: (1) challenge all costly customer requirements; (2) provide sensitivity analyses showing the impact on cost of variations in each of these requirements; (3) emphasize the positive aspects of LCC—engineering, logistics, and planning—rather than the legalistic, protective, contractual factors; (4) use such techniques as level-of-repair analysis and DTC as part of the LCC program. An aggressive LCC effort provides more protection from an accusation of contractual default than a squad of lawyers does.

An incentive clause will benefit the contractor who produces the better product. Therefore, if he has strong innovative abilities, an incentive clause is desirable for the contractor.

Control Risk

The management of risk is the essence of LCC. The buyer and the contractor must share risk in a rational and equitable manner, each assuming those risks he can minimize.

Buyer. Contractual arrangements should seek to ensure the progressive transfer of risk to the contractor during the life of the program. The contract should set limits on the various elements of LCC, progressively tightening them as the element is defined and becomes subject to the contractor's control. The contractor may never be able to control some cost elements, e.g., medical costs of user personnel and retirement benefits, and any risks attached to changes in these costs will remain the buyer's responsibility. Contracts should always require strenuous efforts by the contractor but should not exceed his capabilities (or the price for the excessive demand will, and should, be exorbitant).

Contractor. The assumption of contractual obligation for an LCC element requires the analysis of the risk involved. The contractor takes this risk into account in setting a price, recognizing that an LCC program generates planning, design, logistics, and other work as well as LCC activities. On the other hand, he also realizes that a product with a low LCC will sell better and longer and will have a greater profit potential. Thus, a contractor may respond quite favorably to a demanding contractual requirement for LCC control and will find it counterproductive to seek to evade responsibility for LCC control through contractual devices.

Contractors may diminish the risk in an incentive/penalty clause of a contract by sharing parts of the requirement with subcontractors. Even if most of the apparent responsibility can be assigned to subcontractors, substantial risk remains with the prime contractor for problems that occur at the interfaces between subcontractors.

Understand Gaming

Satisfactory contracts are the result of both parties' efforts to achieve a common understanding of the tasks to be done. Despite sincere attempts to avoid an adversary relationship in contractual negotiations, situations may deteriorate and result in efforts for unilateral advantage. This maneuvering is called *gaming* and may result in a short-term advantage for one party. Almost always, however, the long-term result is trouble for both parties (and in a government monopsony situation, particularly bad trouble for the contractor). Because such gaming is destructive, both parties should be aware that it occurs and should avoid creating conditions that encourage it.

Buyer. One form of contractor gaming is to bid low on a production contract, in the hope of profiting on subsequent tasks, such as modification efforts, spares, training, and so on. LCC procurement is intended to penalize such maneuvers but may stimulate others; the LCC estimate may be made low purposely by underestimates or by omitting cost elements. Contractors must know in advance that the buyer will enforce penalty clauses for LCC overruns. Although enforcement even to the point of bankrupting the contractor will not get the desired product at the desired price, such determination will surely deter unrealistic bids made in the hope of future corrective manipulations.

Contractor. Deliberate (or even inadvertent) vagueness in stating requirements is a common form of gaming by buyers. In a monopsony, they hope to force the contractor to perform more work than was contemplated at the time of contract execution. The cure, again, is to reach a clear agreement during contract negotiations.

Astute contractors recognize the advantage of a long-range view in working with the government. The dual pressures of beating competitors' bids and minimizing financial loss are no different in LCC procurement than in other, more conventional competitions. In LCC procurement, however, the challenge may extend across many years and require greater sensitivity and insight into the customer's (user's) world. Such understanding can lessen the contractor's risk in LCC procurement and provide long-range profitability. When government buyers find that a contractor competently meets the letter and intent of a contract, they will be eager to select that contractor for future business.

Control LCC

Both the buyer and the contractor must organize properly to control LCC; they should assign an individual the authority and responsibility to implement control. That person must be able to integrate LCC activities with all of the program's other functions.

Buyer. As discussed in Chapter 10, after the contract has been signed, the buyer must remain vigilant to see that the

LCC effort is effective. Even before selecting the contractor, the buyer must prepare LCC estimates for competitive alternative choices in the same manner as will be done later for competitive procurement. These estimates are used for budgeting and planning and should be reviewed periodically.

During the life of the program, the buyer should respond positively to all suggestions for changes that will permit reductions in LCC. Provide an initial model for LCC, and develop and expand it as the program grows. Be flexible about the details of LCC but adamant about the total cost goal.

A highly effective method of controlling LCC is to maintain competition as long as possible. During the conceptual phase, consider many means of satisfying the operational need, including the ideas of contractors, government laboratories, and users. During development, maintain competition between two or more contractors (including, possibly, governmental facilities). During production, the amount bought each year from each source can be adjusted on the basis of cost (either production cost or LCC). Of course, competition can seem costly, as the incremental cost of another source is obvious. The savings resulting from competition are apt to be much larger, but less obvious, than the incremental cost of an additional source, so that this trade-off must be very carefully evaluated. Even if a schedule has to be delayed in order to obtain competition, the loss in time may be made up by more aggressive contractor effort.

Contractor. Understanding the customer's real requirements is the key to controlling LCC. A printed requirement for some high degree of performance may represent only the wish of a single individual. Such requirements should be questioned and alternatives suggested if they significantly affect LCC. Good salesmanship means doing this without arrogance and without offense.

Internal and subcontractor control requires the same management attention from the contractor as from the customer.

Do not expect that last-minute compilations for customer reviews will substitute for management's regular involvement with design and planning cost control.

To succeed in a competitive situation, a contractor must develop a unique cost advantage. Only rarely will this advantage come from an estimating method that displays a lower cost. Usually, and more constructively, the advantage results from a better design, a better production scheme, or a more efficient logistic concept. Of course, the estimating method must accurately evaluate these "improvements." For example, if common parts can be used for two or more products, the cost estimates must show the reduction to the designers and the customer and its effect during design, production, and operation.

The trade-offs between performance, DTC, and LCC must continue throughout the program. Frequent reviews of goals and controls will assure the achievement of the lowest possible LCC.

Realize the Potential Savings

Will the projected savings in work loads or procurement promised by LCC analysis be realized in the form of decreased budgets, fewer personnel, and smaller procurements? Or will institutional rigidities block the planned innovations? Every change envisioned by an LCC estimate will take hard work to push it through multiple layers of user indifference or opposition. This is true for governmental, industrial, and consumer users. Each innovation must be explained and discussed. Involve the user with the creation and implementation of such innovations. A "maintenance on demand" system may decrease the need for depot personnel, but such people will not be taken off the payroll unless depot management is properly motivated. A new computer-controlled automobile carburetor will realize its potential fuel savings only if all the drivers, maintenance men, and dealers understand the objective and work to achieve it. Entrenched bureaucracy is not just the burden of government.[1] As another example, standardization should achieve savings in the cost of spares, but these must be realized by the provisioning team and implemented in the field; otherwise, spares of the same common part may not be pooled for multiple use and may even be given a different stock number for each different use.

As a last resort, even if LCC efforts do not allow an institution to save money by reducing its personnel or closing unneeded facilities, they may still increase the institution's capability by allowing it to free personnel and facilities for other tasks, which may be the equivalent of a cost saving.

Provide Complete LCC Estimates

In an advocacy position, users, program offices, and contractors always face the temptation to minimize the LCC estimate. Nevertheless, the LCC model should seek to include all significant costs that the program will incur so as to minimize later unpleasant surprises. (No matter how diligent and intelligent the estimator, some surprises are inevitable.)

Buyer. Many invariant costs allocated to a program will continue whether or not the program survives. For budgeting or forecasting purposes, such costs must be included in the LCC estimate. For comparative purposes, these constant costs (e.g., base maintenance and utility services, or patients, prisoners, and transients) can be omitted and the estimating effort saved.

Include the ultimate user and the potential contractor in the development of the model. Provide incentives for them to offer suggestions. Do not penalize a contractor for adding the cost of a task that others overlooked; such reminders may be unpleasant at the time but will forestall later, even more unpleasant, problems. Provisioning, for example, is often poorly estimated, as is the cost of changes and modifications.

Contractor. The lowest LCC estimate does not always receive the most favorable evaluation by the customer (but it might). Follow the customer's model insofar as possible. If some necessary task has been omitted from the suggested model, note the required addition and consider adding only a nominal amount or zero for the task with an explanatory footnote so as not to make the LCC estimate conspicuously higher than that of the competition. Some evaluators may look only at the bottom line.

Throughout a program, the earlier a cost is recognized, the better for all concerned. The temptation to defer such recognition (so as to avoid raising the estimate) should be resisted at all but the most critical junctures (e.g., immediately prior to a legislative hearing) and then for as short a time as possible.

Get Good Data

Buyer. The user accumulates cost data for reasons other than controlling LCC. The data on reliability, maintainability, and logistics are rarely recorded in the form needed for LCC estimating. If the user can be sufficiently involved in the LCC control process, he will provide data useful for the LCC effort. If he has not collected such data, it may be necessary to set up a separate accounting system, perhaps on a sampling basis. If contractors could recover the cost of data gathering, they could act as such an extra accounting system.

If each buyer could be persuaded to publish the LCC estimates (with backup data) received in competitive procurements after selecting the winner, both buyers and contractors would benefit. All would have access to a library of materials in the public domain of "generally accepted LCC principles and data" for future work.

Buyers should be careful not to ask for data that they do not need. If they do not examine and use such data, the sender will quickly become aware that shortcomings have gone undetected. All subsequent submittals will deteriorate. Worse, the buyer may find that the unread data contained warnings that relieve the sender of subsequent responsibility for an incipient problem.

Contractor. The needed data are available, even when they seem most remote. Discovery takes diligent work and analysis. Customer-provided data may be questionable and should often be revised by the contractor. Usually, the buyer will welcome such corrections, for he knows how weak the data sources are.[2]

Develop New Methods

Although it will always be difficult to estimate the costs of future situations, the estimating methodology needs continuous efforts to improve it. All of the techniques described in this book are tentative and have been advanced only as the best available at this time. Each user of LCC must expand, develop, modify, and improve them. The following points are particularly in need of refinement.

1. The relation between schedule and cost seems especially difficult; an analytic technique is available only for volume production. There are no general methods applicable to development work, testing, or construction. Even worse, after the first estimate, all schedule changes, regardless of whether they shorten or lengthen the time, seem to increase costs. Why?

2. Estimators request information about manufacturing plans, logistics plans, and so on, which logically should affect costs. Yet, to be realistic, most estimators do not use much of this information. Given the relevance of the information to the estimate, how can the estimator include this background in the estimating process? A logic similar to the Bayesian approach to statistics, which quantifies the value of a priori knowledge, might be useful. In this case, it may be possible to quantify the divergence of the new plan from the

plans of analogous programs, which are used as a basis for the estimate.

3. To what extent should estimates be based on current institutional arrangements (the "will cost" estimate), and when should the estimate assume improved arrangements (the "should cost" estimate)? When, for example, orders for spares provisioning are placed at the same time as production orders, the cost of spares may be much lower than when bought after production has stopped. However, in most past procurements, the procurement agency has not been able to buy the spares with production. The LCC analyst should prepare the estimate on the basis of past practice (will cost) and provide a footnote describing the alternative method and its cost impact (should cost).

4. Computer software development and maintenance costs are new and changing. The constant change in computer technology exacerbates the problem. Methods are needed to estimate costs for computers from microprocessors to mainframe machines.

5. LCC models still show inadequate sensitivity to changes in reliability and maintainability. To some extent, these models reflect a real-world situation; innovations in reliability and maintainability are not fully reflected in training, manuals, provisioning, manning, test equipment, and facilities of some programs. Such time lags in realizing the benefits of improved characteristics may have sharp effects on cost estimates. For example, even if a product's reliability or maintainability has been greatly improved, maintenance manpower planners may be reluctant to decrease capability for fear that the advertised improvement may not be effective in use. Because of such reluctance to cut manpower, estimated cost reductions will not happen. Interestingly enough, the maintenance manpower planners may be able to decrease the manning on subsequent programs, after they have seen a real decrease in work load. The benefits of one program's improvements finally affect later programs. An improved

understanding of these relationships could show large changes in both estimating and actual costs.

6. The use of discounting has gone in and out of favor a number of times in the past twenty years. Even the theoretical foundations of discounting are shaky. A definitive solution acceptable to both academic economists and pragmatic legislators is needed.

7. The models used for LCC tend to be comprehensive rather than accurate. There is as yet no method that would allow us to say, "Use this CER only if it will develop a significant amount of cost. Otherwise, do not bother." It should be possible to make this judgment before doing all the work needed to determine that the cost is insignificant. Finally, the judgment must be protected from those critics who point out that a cost was omitted.

8. Even though some existing contractual methods of controlling LCC are better than those in common practice, further developments in contractual techniques are desirable. More thought should be given to (a) various means of placing limits on LCC very early in the development process, by agreements between the using agency and the procuring agency and between the procuring agency and the contractor; (b) ways of increasing the motivation of both the procuring agency and the contractor to reduce costs that they influence or control; (c) contractual incentives to detect and reduce those requirements of the user that generate more costs than they are worth; and (d) the maintenance of competition between alternative systems and contractors during the entire development and procurement process while minimizing the cost of duplication. Together, these should ensure that the user receives a product with a minimum LCC, that the contractor makes a predictable profit, and that both are exposed only to an acceptable risk in this probabilistic, uncertain world.

Summary

1. Obtaining the maximum benefit from limited resources is the goal of LCC; this must be balanced with other program goals to assure success.

2. Control of LCC is a continuing program requirement for buyer and seller. Although ongoing reviews are important, competition is the most effective tool.

3. Both buyer and seller will have to work hard to convert the potential savings of an LCC estimate to actual cost savings. Follow through on estimated cost savings to assure that they are implemented in the program.

4. Risk should be progressively transferred from buyer to seller, as the cost elements become sufficiently defined for the seller to control the risk.

5. Good data are hard to get, but they are indispensable for reliable estimates.

6. An LCC estimate should be continuously revised to make it more complete and more reliable.

7. As in all developing and competitive fields, an investment in additional research can yield high rewards in program success.

Notes

1. William A. Niskanen, Jr., *Bureaucracy and Representative Government* (Chicago: Aldine, 1971) provides the best analysis of the behavior of bureaucracy both in and out of government.

2. Marco R. Fiorello, "Getting 'Real' Data for Life Cycle Costing," *Proceedings of the IEEE 1974 Electronics and Aerospace Conference* (Washington, D.C.: Institute of Electrical and Electronic Engineers, 1974).

Glossary

Most terms in the text are defined upon first use, but for convenience, the definitions are repeated here. A number of U.S. military specifications provide definitions of terms used in LCC. They include:

MIL-STD-280	"Definitions of Item Levels, Item Exchangeability, Models and Related Terms."
MIL-STD-480	"Configuration Control—Engineering Changes, Deviations and Waivers."
MIL-STD-721	"Definitions of Effectiveness Terms for Reliability, Maintainability, Human Factors and Safety."
MIL-STD-881	"Work Breakdown Structures for Defense Material Items."
MIL-STD-1367	"Packaging, Handling, Storage and Transportability Program Requirements."
MIL-STD-1388-1&2	"Logistic Support Analysis."

JCS Pub. 1   "Dictionary of Military and
                              Associated Terms."

These specifications may be obtained from the U.S. Government Printing Office or the Department of Defense, Washington, D.C.

Analogy: a method of estimating on the basis of the similarities between two or more programs.

Availability: a measure of the probability of an item being in an operable state at an unknown (random) point in time.

Award fee: a contractual provision by which the customer determines the fee paid to the contractor on the basis of performance during the contract.

Built-in test: test equipment built into the prime equipment for the detection and isolation of equipment failures.

Cost drivers: the controllable design or planning system characteristics that have a predominant effect on the system's cost.

Cost effectiveness: a measure of the benefits to be derived from, and the resources to be expended on, a system.

Cost element: the building block of cost estimates; the individual cost, defined by all of the descriptors of cost, such as the WBS, subdivision of work, elements of cost, program phase, time, and so on.

Cost-estimating relation: a mathematical expression relating cost as the dependent variable to one or more independent variables.

Cost factor: a brief arithmetic expression wherein cost is determined by the application of a factor as a proportion.

Depot maintenance: maintenance performed in fixed or semifixed installations capable of major overhaul, minor fabrication of parts, and complete overhaul of subassemblies and end items. Similar to factory maintenance. The repaired items are usually returned to inventory.

Design to cost: a management concept wherein rigorous cost goals are established during development and the control of system costs (acquisition, operating, and support) to those goals is achieved by practical trade-offs between operational capability, peformance, cost, and schedule.

Design to cost goals: a specific cost, in constant dollars, based upon a specified production quantity and rate, established early during system development as a management objective and design parameter for subsequent phases of the acquisition cycle.

Direct costs: costs identified to a specific item and charged to that item; distinguished from indirect costs, which are charged to overhead. Allocated direct costs could be identified to a specific product, but because of the cost of record keeping are allocated in accordance with some other measure of product cost.

Discounting (discounted value): the method of computing the present worth of a future expenditure or income.

$$\text{Present worth} = \frac{A}{(1 + i)^n}$$

where

$i =$ discount rate or interest per period

$n =$ number of periods in the future

$A =$ expenditure or income

In government decisions, the nominal discount rate represents the return that would be earned if the money were retained by the private sector. See also *present value.*

Failure rate: the number of failures of an item per unit measure of life (cycles, time, miles, events, and so on).

General and administrative cost: the cost of general management, public relations, legal, and so on, not identified with a particular operating department.

Incentives contract: a contractual device providing additional payments or penalties to the seller for performance above or below the specified requirements.

Industrial engineering estimates: a cost estimate made by summing the cost estimates of the individual parts or components of the whole task; these individual estimates are often made by the persons who will do those component tasks. Also known as grass roots or bottom up estimating.

Inflation, monetary: a period of rising prices for goods and services. It is measured as the ratio between the price of an item at one date and its price at a later date.

Initial operational capability: the date when a system is first deployed and capable of performing its required mission.

Initial spares: those spares procured at the beginning of a program, usually concurrently with the initial procurement of the product, and used to provide a stock at the various supply locations. See also *replenishment spares.*

Integrated logistic support: a composite of all the support considerations necessary to assure the effective and economical support of a system for its life cycle. The principal elements of ILS are: (1) the maintenance plan (2) support and test equipment plan, (3) supply support, (4) transportation and handling, (5) technical data, (6) facilities, (7) personnel and training, (8) logistic support resources funds, and (9) logistics support management information.

Intermediate maintenance: maintenance done by a maintenance organization on another organization's equipment at either a fixed or a mobile facility. The repaired item is returned to the user. The repair work is more complex than the work at organizational level and less complex than that done at a depot.

Life cycle cost: the total cost for an item of research and development, production, modification, transportation, introduction into the inventory, construction, operation, support, maintenance, disposal, salvage revenue, and any other cost of ownership.

Life cycle costing: the consideration of life cycle cost in choices or decisions among different courses of action.

Logistics: the art and science of management, engineering, and technical activities concerned with the support requirements of operational systems including test and support equipment, spares and repair parts, personnel and training, transportation and handling, facilities, and technical data.

Logistic support analysis: a composite of systematic actions taken to identify, define, analyze, quantify, and process logistic support requirements.

Logistic support cost warranty: a contractual guarantee, usually with incentives and penalties, of the logistic support cost of an item. The cost is usually measured by a simulation of the support situation.

Maintainability: a characteristic of design and installation that is expressed as the probability that an item will be retained in or restored to an operable condition within a specified period of time. Also, the activity to assure the achievement of a desired level of this probability.

Maintenance: all action taken to retain material in a serviceable condition or to restore it to serviceability. It includes inspection, testing, servicing, repair, rebuilding, and reclamation.

Manufacturing plan: the methods of tooling, fabrication, assembly, and test, with schedules, flow charts, personnel requirements, and facilities and equipment.

Manufacturing planning: the detailed operations sheets containing instructions for the workman for fabrication, assembly, or test and listing the tools, materials, and equipment to be used.

Mean time between failures (MTBF): the average time interval between item failures during the constant failure period of an item's life. It is measured by the total number of failures divided by the time interval; it is equal to the reciprocal of the failure rate. MTBF is also expressed in cycles, miles, events, or other measures of life units.

Mean time to repair (MTTR): the average time required to repair an item. It is measured by dividing the total corrective maintenance time by the total number of corrective maintenance actions during a given period of time.

Mission need: a required capability within an agency's overall purpose, including cost and schedule considerations. See also *operational requirement.*

Model: a cost model is a set of mathematical rules, a computer program, if used, and data to estimate costs based on technical and programmatic parameters.

Nonrecurring costs: fixed costs, such as tooling, test equipment, and planning, which are generally independent of the quantity to be produced or tested.

Operating and support: the program phase during which the product is used. The phase is initiated by acceptance of the product and includes all operations, maintenance, and modification; O&S costs include charges for personnel, provisioning, fuel, support equipment, and manuals for maintenance and operations. Sometimes referred to as the operations and maintenance phase.

Operating and support cost: those resources necessary to operate and support a system during its useful life in the inventory.

Organizational maintenance: maintenance authorized for, performed by, and the responsibility of, a using organization on its own equipment.

Parametric methods: estimating methods based on common attributes of two or more programs, such as weight, power, or speed.

Present value (also present discounted value): the algebraic sum of the value of a stream of expenditures and/or income, discounted to the present time.

$$PV = \frac{A}{(1 + i)^{n_1}} + \frac{B}{(1 + i)^{n_2}} + \frac{C}{(1 + i)^{n_3}} + \text{etc.}$$

where

PV	=	Present value
i	=	Discount rate or interest per period
n_x	=	Number of periods in the future
A, B, C	=	Expenditure or income per period

See also *discounting.*

PRICE (Programmed Review of Information for Costing and Evaluation): a computer program that calculates development and production costs for hardware based on the physical characteristics. Proprietary, developed by Frank Freiman, RCA, Inc. Cherry Hill, N.J.

Recurring costs: repetitive costs incurred for each item or each time period of production or test or use. Usually expressed as a cost per item or a cost per month.

Redundancy: the existence of more than one means for accomplishing a given function. Each means of accomplishing the function need not be identical.

Reliability improvement warranty: a fixed-price contractual incentive for operational reliability and maintainability improvement providing for contractor repair of failed material over a stated period of time.

Replenishment spares: those spares intended to replace items used for the repair of equipment or the loss of equipment. See also *initial spares.*

Risk: the possible variability in an estimate or plan expressed quantitatively or narratively; technical, schedule, and cost risks are usually expressed quantitatively with limits at various probabilities.

Sensitivity analysis: the determination of the impact on the final result of a change in the input variables, individually or in concert.

Should cost: an estimate of costs based on an optimum situation envisioned by the cost analyst. Cf. *will cost.*

Software: a set of computer programs, data bases, procedures, rules, and associated documentation concerned with the operation of a data processing system.

Sunk costs: those expenditures already made or irrevocably committed.

Support equipment: the tools, test equipment, trucks, generators, work stands, calibration apparatus, and so on needed to operate and maintain a system.

System: a composite of equipment, skills, and techniques capable of performing or supporting an operational role. Item levels from the simplest division to the more complex are: part, subassembly, assembly, unit, group, set, subsystem, and system.

System effectiveness: the degree to which a system can be expected to perform its mission requirements while operating in the external environment. It is a function of the system's availability, dependability, and capability.

System engineering: the process that transforms an operational need (mission requirement) into a description of a system performance parameters (design requirements) and a preferred system configuration.

Target logistic support cost: a cost goal established for contractual purposes expressed as the sum of specified and defined logistic support elements. When used for incentive purposes, the cost elements are selected on the basis of being controllable by the contractor's decisions. See also *logistic support cost warranty.*

Terotechnology: a combination of management, financial, engineering, and other practices applied to physical assets in pursuit of economic life cycle costs. For further information, contact The National Terotechnology Centre, Cleeve Road, Leatherhead, Surrey KT22 7SA, England.

Unit flyaway (rollaway, sailaway) cost: the average unit flyaway cost includes the cost of the basic unit fabricated, nonrecurring costs, installed customer-furnished equipment, and an allowance for engineering change orders.

Will cost: an estimate of costs based on present institutional arrangements; the expected cost if the state of the world is not changed. Cf. *should cost.*

Work breakdown structure: a product-oriented family tree composed of hardware, services, and data that results from project engineering efforts during the development and production of a defense material item and that completely defines the product(s) to be developed or produced and relates the elements of work to be accomplished to each other and to the end product.

Bibliography

Balaban, Harold S., and Meth, Martin A. "Contractor Risk Associated with Reliability Improvement Warranty." *Proceedings of the 1978 Annual Reliability and Maintainability Symposium*. New York: Institute of Electrical and Electronic Engineers, 1978.

Bazovsky, Igor. *Reliability Theory and Practice*. Englewood Cliffs, N.J.: Prentice-Hall, 1961.

Blanchard, Benjamin S. *Design and Manage to Life Cycle Cost*. Forest Grove, Oreg.: M/A Press, 1978.

———. *Logistics Engineering and Management*. Englewood Cliffs, N.J.: Prentice-Hall, 1974.

Blanchard, Benjamin S., and Lowery, E. E. *Maintainability Principles and Practices*. New York: McGraw-Hill, 1969.

Boardman, Thomas J., and Bryson, Maurice C. "A Review of Some Smoothing and Forecasting Techniques." *Journal of Quality Technology* 10 (1978): 1-11.

Box, George E. P., and Jenkins, Gwilyn M. *Time Series Analysis: Forecasting and Control*. San Francisco: Holden-Day, 1970.

Building Construction Cost Data. Duxbury, Mass.: Robert Snow Means Co., 1977.

Burrington, Richard Stevens, and May, Donald Curtis, Jr.

Handbook of Probability and Statistics with Tables. New York: McGraw-Hill, 1970.

Clark, Rolf H. "Should Defense Managers Discount Future Costs?" *Defense Management Journal,* March 1978, pp. 12-14.

Collins, Dwight E. *Analysis of Available Life Cycle Cost Models and Their Applications.* Wright-Patterson Air Force Base, Ohio: Joint AFSC/AFLC Commanders' Working Group on Life Cycle Cost, June 1976.

Current Construction Costs. Walnut Creek, Calif.: Lee Saylor, 1977.

Dix, Donald M., and Riddel, Fred R. "Projecting Cost-Performance Trade-Offs for Military Vehicles." *Astronautics and Aeronautics,* September 1976, pp. 40-49.

English, J. Morley, ed. *Cost-Effectiveness: The Economic Evaluation of Engineered Systems.* New York: Wiley, 1968.

Fiorello, Marco R. "Getting 'Real' Data for Life Cycle Costing." *Proceedings of the IEEE 1974 Electronics and Aerospace Conference.* Washington, D.C.: Institute of Electrical and Electronic Engineers, 1974.

Fiorello, Marco R., and Jones, Lester G., Jr. *Combat Vehicle System Operating and Support Costs: Guidelines for Analysis.* Washington, D.C.: Logistics Management Institute, June 1977.

Fisher, Gene H. *Cost Considerations in Systems Analysis.* New York: American Elsevier, 1971.

Fleischer, Gerald A., ed. *Risk and Uncertainty: Non-Deterministic Decision Making in Engineering Economy.* Norcross, Ga.: Engineering Economy Division, American Institute of Industrial Engineers, 1975.

Gabel, Grant E. "Capitalizing on Cost-Reducing Opportunities." *Defense Management Journal,* January 1977.

Gallagher, Paul F. *Project Estimating by Engineering Methods.* New York: Hayden Book, 1965.

General Construction Estimating Standards. Solana Beach,

Calif.: Richardson Engineering Services, 1977.

Gobis, Carl J. *Tool, Die and Industrial Estimating: Estimators Handbook.* Detroit, Mich.: Estimators Handbook, 1968.

Grant, Eugene L., and Ireson, Grant W. *Principles of Engineering Economy.* New York: Ronald Press, 1970.

Haley, Charles W., and Schall, Lawrence D. *The Theory of Financial Decisions.* New York: McGraw-Hill, 1973.

Hinrichs, Major General Frank A. "Design to Cost Requires Common Understanding, Clear Direction." *Defense Management Journal,* July 1974.

Jelen, F.C. *Cost and Optimization Engineering.* New York: McGraw-Hill, for the American Association of Cost Engineers, 1970.

"Life Cycle Cost." *Defense Management Journal,* January 1976.

Light Construction Estimating and Engineering Standards. Solana Beach, Calif.: Richardson Engineering Services, 1977.

Mabert, Vincent A. "An Introduction to Short-Term Forecasting Using Box-Jenkins Methodology." Norcross, Ga.: Production Planning and Control Division, American Institute of Industrial Engineers, 1975.

Mark, R. K., and Stuart-Alexander, D. E. "Disaster as a Necessary Part of Benefit-Cost Analysis." *Science,* September 16, 1977.

Metzger, Philip W. *Managing a Programming Project.* Englewood Cliffs, N.J.: Prentice-Hall, 1973.

Miller, Irwin, and Freund, John E. *Probability and Statistics for Engineers.* Englewood Cliffs, N.J.: Prentice-Hall, 1965.

Muckstadt, John A., and Pearson, John M. *MOD METRIC: A Multi-Echelon, Multi-Indenture Inventory Model.* Wright-Patterson Air Force Base, Ohio: Air Force Logistics Command, June 1972.

Nelson, J.P. *Life Cycle Analysis of Aircraft Turbine Engines: Executive Summary.* R-2103/1-AF. Santa Monica, Calif.: The Rand Corp., 1977.

Niskanen, William A., Jr. *Bureaucracy and Representative Government.* Chicago: Aldine, 1971.

Ostwald, Phillip. *Cost Estimating for Engineering and Management.* Englewood Cliffs, N.J.: Prentice-Hall, 1974.

Raiffa, Howard, and Schlaiffer, Robert. *Applied Statistical Decision Theory.* Cambridge, Mass.: Harvard University Press, 1961.

Reynolds, Smith, and Hills, Architects-Engineers-Planners, Inc. *Life Cycle Costing Emphasizing Energy Conservation: Guidelines for Investment Analysis.* Jacksonville, Fla.: Reynolds, Smith, and Hills for ERDA, 1977.

Seiler, Carl. *Introduction to Systems Cost Effectiveness.* New York: Wiley, 1969.

Shillinglaw, Gordon. *Cost Accounting: Analysis and Control.* Homewood, Ill.: Irwin, 1972.

Shishko, Robert. *Choosing the Discount Rate for Defense Decision Making.* Santa Monica, Calif.: The Rand Corp., 1976.

Solomon, Kenneth A., and Okrent, David. "Hazard Prevention." *Journal of the System Safety Society,* January/February 1975.

Taha, Hamdy A. *Operations Research: An Introduction.* New York: Macmillan, 1971.

Trigg, Clifton T. *Guidelines for Cost Estimation by Analogy,* ECOM-4125. Ft. Monmouth, N.J.: U.S. Army Electronics Command, 1973.

Trucks, H. E. *Designing for Economical Production.* Dearborn, Mich.: Society of Manufacturing Engineers, 1974.

Tucker, Stephen A. *Cost-Estimating and Pricing with Machine Hour Rates.* Englewood Cliffs, N.J.: Prentice-Hall, 1962.

U.S. Air Force. *USAF Cost and Planning Factors,* AFR 173-10, vols. 1-2. Washington, D.C.: Department of the Air Force, 1977.

U.S. Air Force. *Engineering Management* MIL-STD-499A (USAF). Washington, D.C.: U.S. Air Force, 1974.

U.S. Air Force. *Handbook for the Implementation of the Design to Cost Concept,* SA-TR 75-2. Kirtland Air Force Base, N.M.: Directorate of Aerospace Studies, 1975.

U.S. Army, Comptroller of the Army, Directorate of Cost Analysis. *Army Force Planning Cost Handbook.* Washington, D.C.: Department of the Army, 1977.

U.S. Army. *Standards for Presentation and Documentation of Life Cycle Cost Estimates for Army Material Systems,* Pamphlet No. 11-5. Washington, D.C.: Department of the Army, 1976.

U.S. Department of Defense, Joint Logistics Commanders Guide to Design-to-Cost. *Life Cycle Cost as a Design Parameter,* DARCOM P700-6, NAVMAT P5242, AFLCP/ AFSCP 800-19. Washington, D.C.: Department of Defense, 1977.

U.S. Department of Defense. *Design to Cost,* Directive 5000.28. Washington, D.C.: Department of Defense, 1975.

———. *Development of Integrated Logistic Support for Systems/Equipment,* Directive 4100.35. Washington, D.C.: Department of Defense, 1970.

———. *Logistic Support Analysis.* MIL-STD-1388-1 and -2. Washington, D.C.: Department of Defense, 1973.

———. *Maintainability Prediction,* MIL-HDBK-472. Washington, D.C.: Department of Defense, 1975.

———. *Work Breakdown Structure for Defense Material Items,* MIL-STD-881. Washington, D.C.: Department of Defense, 1975.

U.S. Executive Office of the President, Office of Management and Budget. *Major Systems Acquisition,* Bulletin A 109, April 5, 1976.

U.S. Executive Office of the President, Office of Management and Budget, Office of Federal Procurement Policy. *Major Systems Acquisition: A Discussion of the Application of OMB Circular No. A-109,* Pamphlet no. 1, August, 1976.

U.S. General Accounting Office. *Ways to Make Greater Use of the Life Cycle Costing Acquisition Technique in DOD,*

B-178214. Washington, D.C.: GAO, May 21, 1973.

——. *Theory and Practice of Cost Estimating for Major Acquisitions*, B-163058. Washington, D.C.: GAO, July 24, 1972.

U.S. Navy. *Navy Program Factors Manual.* OPNAV 90P-02, vols. 1-2. Philadelphia: Naval Publications and Forms Center, 1977.

——. *Requirements for Digital Computer Program Documentation*, WS-8506, rev. 1. Washington, D.C.: Department of the Navy, November 1, 1971.

Urien, René. "Some Thoughts about the Economic Justification of Life Cycle Costing Formulae." *Industrialization Forum* 6 (1975).

Vernon, Ivan R. *Realistic Cost Estimating for Manufacturing.* Dearborn, Mich.: American Society of Tool and Manufacturing Engineers, 1968.

Weimer, David C. *An Assessment of Goal Achievement for the Initial Electronic Subsystem Design-To-Cost Experiments*, P-1239. Washington, D.C.: Insitute for Defense Analyses, December 1976.

——. *The Impact of Reliability Guarantees and Warranties on Electronic Subsystem Design and Development Programs*, S-483. Washington, D.C.: Institute for Defense Analyses, October 1976.

Index